Through Mirdite in Winter

Stavre Th. Frasheri

Translated into English from the original in Albanian
by
Peter R. Prifti

East European Monographs, Boulder
Distributed By Columbia University Press, New York
2002

EAST EUROPEAN MONOGRAPHS, NO. DLXCVI

ISBN: 0-88033-494-0
Library of Congress Control Number: 2002101922

The original title in Albanian:
Përmes Mirditës në Dimër (Through Mirdite in Winter)
The Peppo-Marko Press, Korçë (Albania), 1930

Printed in the United States of America

Contents

Acknowledgements

While working on the translation of *Through Mirdite in Winter* in 1979, I had the privilege to work closely with Prof. Richard C. Bartlett, then Director of Publications at Harvard University's Peabody Museum of Archaeology and Ethnology. He had a gracious way of encouraging me throughout the process of translation. Twenty years later, I had the good fortune to work with Tim Cullen in his capacity of Manager of Publication at Peabody. It was he who gave "the green light," so to speak, for the publication of the English translation, believing that it made more sense to publish the manuscript, than to let it rest in the Peabody repository (where it was placed, after I completed the translation).

Thanks are due to Philip Hubbard, Professor of Linguistics, for his assistance in the preparation of the Glossary of Albanian words and phrases; and to S. Van Christo, currently President of the Frosina Information Network in Boston, who took a lively interest in the manuscript from the start and made vigorous efforts to publicize it.

I wish to note here the helpful comments and suggestions regarding the manuscript, of two other scholars: Joel Halpern, Professor of Anthropology at the University of Massachusetts in Amherst; and Antonia Young, Research Associate in Anthropology at Colgate University, Hamilton, New York.

While researching the book, I benefited from consultations with Sulejman Spata, Tomor Zavalani, and Gjon Pepaj regarding the idiom and customs of Mirditë.

To Naum Prifti, renowned Albanian author of books of short stories, plays, children's fables, etc., I owe a special debt of gratitude for editing the manuscript. It was a responsibility which he handled with diligence and the skills of a seasoned editor.

My warm appreciation to Rafaela Kondi, a scholar of anthropology, for writing the introduction to the book, which is at the same time a "short essay" that pay tribute to Dr. Carleton S. Coon and Stavre Frasheri.

I acknowledge also the contribution of Julika Prifti who assisted in the typing of the manuscript.

Finally, I have been gratified to work closely with the affable and urbane Prof. Stephen Fischer-Galati, respected editor of the *East European Quarterly,* and Editor of the *East European Monographs* series, an established institution for the diffusion of knowledge.

Peter R. Prifti

Foreword

Stavre Frashëri had no way of knowing that he owed his chance of writing *Through Mirdita In Winter* to the desire of Professor Earnest A. Hooton of Harvard to experience vicarious adventures through the person of one of his students—myself, at first, later to be accompanied by my wife, Mary Goodale Coon. Hooton followed me, and then us, through four expeditions into the Riffian tribes of Morocco, the last of which ended only a year before our trip to Albania, in the Fall of 1929.

Accompanied first by a 1929 Harvard graduate, Frederick E. Farnsworth, and later by Mary, I went to Tirana to visit the ten tribes of feuding and fighting white North Albanian mountaineers living on either side of the twin rivers, the White and Black Drin, and of their tumultuous joint outlet to the Adriatic Sea near Shkodër (Scutari).

My main objective was to measure the Gheg (Giants) with at least 100 men representing each tribe, some Muslim, some Catholic, and others including members of both faiths. I went north from the capital Tirana three times, first with Frederick Farnsworth and Anthony Stevens, a one-armed, horse-riding guide who was a clerk at the US Legation going on holiday to his birthplace in the tribe of Has, then and still a part of Yugoslavia. Our route took us through the eastern Gheg tribes of Puka, Dibra, and Luma to Has. Our second trip, with Mary, who had just arrived, led us through the tribes of Mati and Mirdita into Puka, whence we came down to sea-level via Scutari and returned by automobile to Tirana. Stavre Frashëri was our interpreter on this trip. He had been teaching at an American Missionary School in Durrës (Durazzo) and was allowed leave to go with us. Although a Tosc he was not afraid to travel among the supposedly wild Ghegs who spoke a different dialect or language (a problem we both prefer to leave to linguists).

After our second trip, Mary departed and was replaced by Mr. Farnsworth with Mr. Frashëri continuing as guide-interpreter. We went up the eastern route again, then crossed the Drin into the northerly and least accessible tribes of Malsia e Jakovës, Dukagjin, and Malsia e Madhe. This was a much longer trip than the one to Mirdita but Frashëri says nothing in his book about it except for a few parenthetical anecdotes. It was not easy for Farnsworth or me, both used to climbing snowy mountains, but it must have shaken Frashëri, who took it like a man without complaint.

He credited both Mary and me with knowing only three words of Albanian, meaning "Very good!" and "Have a long life!" He did not seem to know that I had been studying Albanian before we left and understood much more of what was being said that I let on. On the other hand he must have remembered some of the silly things I did and decided to forget them even though my chances of having his book translated were small.

Despite, or perhaps because of, his single-mindedness Stavre Frashëri wrote a remarkably full and enjoyable ethnography of a people and their culture undergoing rapid change, for which we should be forever grateful. Some of his travel scenes, e.g. "the Munella mountain still followed us, as it were, along the way," remind one of George Borrow in his *Wild Wales*, and *A Bible in Spain*. His collection of Gheg poetry, so beautifully rendered by Peter Prifti, is most stimulating, and makes a priceless addition to the corpus of Bronze and Iron Age orally transmitted songs. The men who composed and transmitted these haunting echoes of emotion were our living cultural ancestors, and Frashëri must have known it, although he larded appreciation of them with didactic admonitions directed toward a more felicitous if duller cultural status, under the then temporary regime of the dictatorial Mati tribesman, Ahmed Zogu. Fifty years have passed since Stavre Frashëri wrote. How many of his dreams have come true?

Rumor has reached me that Stavre Frashëri is still alive and teaching. If, as I hope, this it true, I salute him with one of my two Albanian words: "*Tungjatjeta*", meaning "Have a long life!"

As for Peter Prifti, I know that he is alive, and I thank him from the bottom of my ancient heart.

Dr. Carlton Coon
Emeritus Professor
of Anthropology
Harvard University
October 21, 1979

Translator's Note

It was almost 40 years ago, in the summer of 1960, when I first met the central figure in this book, Professor Carleton S. Coon. The place was Boston, and the occasion was the week-long Seminar on Albanian Studies, of the Pan-Albanian Federation of America, known for short as *Vatra* (The Hearth), which I organized in my capacity as secretary of the organization. The seminar was held in the Hilton Hotel in downtown Boston. I had invited Prof. Coon to take part in the seminar as one of the speakers, along with Bishop Fan S. Noli; Prof. Thomas Nassi, foremost Albanian-American musical figure; and Arshi Pipa, writer and literary critic of Albanian background. He accepted without hesitation or conditions, and on the second evening of the seminar delighted the audience with personal anecdotes about his encounters with Albanians, especially of course during his 1929 expedition in Albania.

Naturally, I was gratified by his participation at the seminar, and the enthusiastic reception of his talk. Therefore, when years later, in the Seventies, he asked me id I'd be willing to translate Stavre Frashëri's book *Përmes Mirditës në Dimër*, into English, I said "Yes." I accepted, first of all, to discharge what I felt was an obligation on my part to Prof. Coon in connection with the 1960 Seminar. Secondly, I reasoned that this was an opportunity to make known to English readers the research expedition in my native country of a distinguished Harvard scholar, who had made a worthy contribution to knowledge of the Albanian people in the area of anthropology and related fields.

Several things need to be noted with regard to the translation of Frashëri's book.

Seeing that the author is often overly concise in his style, I took it upon myself to amplify or complete his thought, whenever that seemed advisable, while taking care to remain faithful to the substance of the text.

The name Mirditë, like all Albanian names, has a definite form spelled "Mirdita" (pronounced Meer-DEE-tah, with the accent on the second syllable), and an indefinite one "Mirditë" (pronounced Meer-

DEE-tuh). In this work, the indefinite form "Mirditë" has been used throughout, not only to be consistent, but also because this form is used more widely than the other.

Scattered through the book are a number of Albanian words and phrases, taken from the original text. All of them are accompanied by English translations or, additionally, by footnotes whenever necessary. The rationale for this was to give the reader the flavor, as it were, of the Mirdita idiom. The Glossary of Albanian words and phrases in back of the book is intended as an aid to the pronunciation of such terms. In closing, I shall take the liberty to indulge in a personal reminiscence of Prof. Coon. After I agreed to do the translation, he invited me and Prof. Richard Bartlett (see Acknowledgements) to visit him at his home in Gloucester, Massachusetts. Although he was advanced in years at the time (1977), he retained his gift as a *raconteur* and his sense of humor, and we spent a delightful evening in his company. He took special pleasure in showing us prized souvenirs he had brought back from Mirdita, among them a sturdy hand-carved wooden chair, beautifully designed.

I completed the translation in 1979. Soon after a plan was drawn to publish the manuscript. The plan was not realized, however, in part because Prof. Coon died in 1981 (at the age of 77). He would be delighted, were he alive, to see it published twenty years later.

Peter R. Prifti
San Diego, California
February, 2001

Introduction

When, in the Fall, Winter and Spring of 1929–1930, Professor Carlton S. Coon, accompanied by his wife, visited Albania it was with the stated intention of doing research and writing "a main outline of [Gheg] culture as a whole and only in those details that bear specifically on our problem: who are the Ghegs and how did they acquire their present anatomical characteristics?" It was not until 1950, however, that his book *The Mountains of Giants: A Racial and Cultural Study of the North Albanian Mountain Ghegs* was published. During that expedition Stavre Frasheri acted as the Coons' guide and interpreter. He also kept his own detailed notes of their trip. Frasheri's account, *Through Mirdite in Winter*, was published in Albania in 1930, shortly after the conclusion of the expedition. His goal, he claimed, was to describe the Highlands of Albania as seen by an Albanian, so as to juxtapose his account to what "comes from travel accounts written by foreign visitors to our country." And although the two books cover some of the same ethnographic territory, the Albanian account is a unique case, for when added to that of Coon, it provides us with two perspectives on the "same" events—that of an outsider, a trained anthropologist, and that of an educated insider exploring this remote and "exotic" part of his country for the first time.

By the 1930s some Albanians had already crossed the Atlantic and others had established communities in Western Europe and as far east as the Black Sea and yet the land north of Shkumbin river within Albania was a mystery. The Highlands were thought of as a land of "primitive" culture, poverty and outlawry. While accompanying Coon, Frasheri used the opportunity to observe and write his own account of the Mirdite social organization, family life, gender roles, cultural values, blood feuds, weddings, death rituals, etc. Both Frasheri and Coon were impressed by the preservation of an old cultural and social system in which "family and kin are the main social units."

Frasheri was attracted to the people of the Mirdite region of the Highlands as they appeared to be the most isolated, most primitive and most distinctive of Highlanders. He noted the names of villages and the routes to them with the same diligence that he described the interiors of residences in which they spent the night. He recorded the names of their hosts and conversation that took place around the table. After treating of the social organization, including the roles of men and women and their occupations, he described the *kulla*, the typical square tower built for defensive purposes. He relied on folk legends to explain how the Mirdite people came to be what they are. In attempting a "portrait" of the Mirdite people, he did not avoid the painful aspects of their lives due to scarcities, nor glimpses of joy. The material and economic scarcity and poverty of life, however, contrasted sharply with an abundance of spiritual and human values. Their lives revolved around granting and receiving honor, hospitality, respect for one's social status and rank, and a fanatical veneration for clergy.

Frasheri, nevertheless, was critical of the low status and condition of women in that society, of the clergy's general indifference and passivity to misery and ignorance, and of the ever-present tragedies resulting from blood-feuds. In the face of these conditions, his objectivity was truly strained. He wished to see life for the Mirdite people improved and ventured his own ideas for their advancement. In his records, among other observations, he noted some significant changes in 1930, in particular the involuntary turning of the gunmen into farmers.

Some of the most pleasant passages to read are moments of watching Professor Coon at work. From Frasheri's narrative it appears that their host would ask the men in a locality to go and be measured, or would give an order to the elders roundabout. "Be measured? But why? ...For army recruitment? Taxes? Labor?... It was with misgivings that they came to be measured, and some even consulted with one another before going through with it." But once the measuring started it attracted a curios crowd and bystanders always ready and quick to crack jokes about the men to be measured.

Coon was the first American physical anthropologist to set foot in Albania with the intention of actually writing a study on the typology of the Albanian Highlander. Undoubtedly he benefited from, as well as added to the literature of other British and American travelers who had trekked to those mountains before him. Even though his theory of typology might be controversial and bypassed or superseded today, *Mountains of Giants* can serve as a reference book to young Albanian anthropologists. Coon's contribution lies in the cultural interpretation of the social and economic implications of Gheg houses, the economics of the production of men's clothing and equipment, the social aspect of smoking etc. His approach was academic, "...smoking...forms a ready means of polite interaction, for men give each other cigarettes...." While Frasheri recorded the actual events: "Our host took out his tobacco box, and rolled a cigarette for each of us to light up...."

The chapter on Greetings and Oaths arouses particular interest. Any greeting however trivial, entails more than a handshake and a quick polite exchange. As Frasheri explains, it involves a solemn touch on both temples, and a lengthy inquiry after one's health, all done with a certain formality. One has to take time when greeting, as a matter that cannot be rushed, nor taken lightly without risking to antagonize the party being greeted. There is a "ritualistic stalling" quality to it, as if to show absence of ill-intentions on both sides. Exchanging health-related questions about family members and offering the right salutation for each answer, assures time for holding at bay rushed decisions and dispelling any suspicions.

Reading Frasheri's travel notes now at the beginning of the 21st century, one finds fascinating details, from the mundane to the portentous that resonate in the present. Their recycling system involved "an opening [near the hearth] for pouring down the dirty water. The waste water makes its way to the barn nearby...." Regarding Mirdite hospitality, Frasheri states: "Whether it is because of their primitive social organization, or the absence of inns and hotels, or the low mobility of the population owing to bad roads, the fact remains that the guest will find an open door everywhere in this region, where he is greeted with the words:

"Welcome, oh friend! God has brought you here, oh friend!"

Frasheri wrote a chapter titled "Bravery" to illustrate the high regard for fighters and respect for death among the highlanders. He notes that "the gun has been their inseparable companion," and to prove the historic companionship, he provides an impressive vocabulary of the military hardware of the Highlands. Yet in the same chapter he includes some powerful lyrics of old folk songs, selected with taste and love for the folklore.

In conclusion, Frasheri tried to capture that "special character" about Mirdite, the deep-seated human qualities, both positive and negative, which once again can be of much interest to travelers and scientists, Albanians and non-Albanians alike.

Following the path of German, Austrian, French, Czech, Danish, and English scholars such as Hahn, Reinhold, Dozon, Jarnik, Pedersen, G. Mayer, Nopsca, Edith Durham, few American authors have written essays or travelers notes of their journeys in Albania. A prominent one in her class was Rose Wilder Lane, author of "The Peaks of Shala," followed by George Fred Williams, "The Albanians." Dr. Coon's book is worthy of special credit since as a well-defined scientific work, it enriched the anthropometrics studies in Albania.

Rafaela Kondi
M.A. in Cultural Anthropology
New York, NY
March 2001

Author's Preface

"Do you know where you are going? You will die of cold there. You will be devoured by wolves and other beasts in those high mountains. You will be mired in six-foot-deep snow. Food is lacking and malaria is rampant."

That's what my friends and relatives would say to me, whenever I mentioned that I was going to the Highlands, along with an American lady and gentleman who where going there to do studies on anthropology.

For many years I had the desire to visit the land of valor in Albania, about which many foreigners had written.

My chance came, and disregarding the dangers that my friends pointed out to me, I gladly agreed to accompany Dr. Carleton Coon and his wife; all the more so when I learned that this delicate woman, though unfamiliar with the terrain, was ready to go to the land of the big snow, wolves and to endure great discomfort.

Few are the Albanians, unfortunately, who take the trouble to visit other parts of Albania. As a result, whatever knowledge they have about the country, comes from travel accounts written by foreign visitors to our country.

We are Albanians, yet we do not know Albania well.

The data given by a foreigner may have the advantage of being impartial. But on the other hand, they may be inaccurate, because of the author's lack of familiarity with our language, as well as our sentiments. Exaggerations, whether in favor or against a country, always detract from the value of a study. For example, what are we to think when a foreigner says that there are men with tails in Albania, or that Albanians live in huts?

In the course of this journey we visited Mirditë, Pukë, Zadrimë, the Highlands, Mat, Selitë, Lurë, Dibër, Lumë, Has, the Highland of Gjakovë, and Dukagjin. We had four beasts of burden—at times only three—to carry our belongings. We made practically the entire journey on foot. Indeed, at one time we were forced to carry our belongings on our back. This happened during a heavy snowfall in

Dukagjin, when our beasts of burden got stuck in the snow, and were unable to take even a single step forward.

Of all the regions we visited, I shall try to describe at some length only Mirditë, which from many viewpoints attracted me above all others. We spent more time in Mirditë than in other places, and as a result I had more time for study there. Moreover, Mirditë is much more distinct than the other regions, it has a special character, plus a social system that is still primitive.

I hope this study will be of interest to those who know nothing about our Highlands, especially southern Albanians and Albanians who live abroad.

When I was in the nation's capital Tiranë, I read a large portion of my manuscript to certain friends of mine from Mirditë. When I finished reading, they said to me: "By God, that's just how it is!"

The Americans were amazed at the great freedom they found in our country, for although they were carrying revolvers in their belts, nobody bothered them about gun permits or other matters. Wherever we went, the people accommodated us, above all the police who helped us in every way.

In conclusion, I wish to express my thanks to the Women's Society of Korçë and the Korçë city administration which contributed much to the publication of this work.

S[tavre] Th. F[rashëri]

Albania

Map of Albania showing principal cities

Northern Albania

Map of northern Albanian showing the Mirdite region and neighboring districts

1

The Origin of the Mirditë People

What is the origin of the Mirditë people? Are they native to the region, or immigrants? These are questions that may well be raised by someone who visits the region for the first time. I, too, tried to learn something about the origin of the inhabitants of this place. The data I give below are not based on books that have been written over the years, but rather on the beliefs of the people of Mirditë.

From questions that have been asked here and there—including questions I asked the *Kapedan*,* of Mirditë—it is believed that the people of Mirditë came to this land during the time of the Marinë King, Marinë being a place that is now under Yugoslav rule. But which king that was, what period they emigrated from there, and what kind of people they found here, is not known. Legend has it that there was a father who had five sons. When the time came for them to separate,[1] their father, seeing that he had no property to give them, handed instead a *shoshë* (sieve) to one, a *shalë* (harness) to the second son, a *shpatë* (sword) to the third, a *hinkë* (funnel) to the fourth, while the fifth son he said to go and rule over Orosh. And so, we have today the localities of Shosh, Shalë, Kuzhnen, Spaç, and Orosh, all of which are bound by fraternal ties, inasmuch as they were founded by brothers, the first two of whom settled in the Dukagjin regions, while the other three settled in Mirditë, as we know it today.

In Shosh they told me that there were not five brothers, but three and that they are represented today by Shalë, Shosh and Mirditë.

One legend says that the name of Mirditë came about this way: A long time ago, the King of the land was at war with his enemies. In his

---

* Kapedan, clan leader, chief. The word is derived from Captain, as used by the military to indicate grade or rank.

1 According to the custom, when brothers of a family living under one roof reached maturity, or for some reason could no longer continue to live together, they divided the family's wealth among themselves, then went their separate ways.

serviçe he had also a few men from the region that is known as Mirditë. The time came to mount the attack. But it chanced that the day on which the attack was to take place was Friday. For this reason the King preferred to put off the attack until a later date.[2]

But the *Kapedan* of Mirditë proposed to the King that he mount the attack that very day, because he would find the enemy unprepared for battle. The King took his advice, the attack was carried out, the enemy was destroyed, and thereafter that day was called *Dita e Mirë* (the Good Day), which later came to be pronounced *Mirë-Dita*, or *Mirditë*, and in time became the name of the entire region that is presently known as Mirditë.

---

2 Friday is a holy day for Muslims, as Sunday is for Christians. And since the inhabitants of this region were Muslims, Friday was for them a day of rest and prayer, rather than war and exertion.

2

The Social Organization

Of all the regions of the Highlands, Mirditë is the only one that still preserves its primitive social system. Although in olden times it was divided politically in different ways, the Mirditë inhabitants have always regarded the five *bajraks* (social-administrative units) of the region as an entity. The five *bajraks* did not have a collective name. However the name of Mirditë stood for all five *bajraks*, which today are known as: Orosh, Spaç, Kuzhnen, Fan, and Dibër. The first three, as we said earlier, are considered as one family; consequently, there are no intermarriages among them.[3] Members of the Fan and Dibër clans, on the other hand, can marry into the other three, since they arrived in the region at a later date.

Family and kin are the main social units, and may include many households, spread over different villages. The people of Mirditë never marry within the clan, even if they are ten generations apart. The clan played an even more important role in questions of blood feuds.

One day, at a house where we had stopped overnight, a policeman told me that the bride of the house was his sister. When I asked him for details, he told me that she was not actually his sister, but a woman belonging to his clan.

Since they do not marry with members of the five *bajraks* in their region, the people of Mirditë marry outside the clan, for example, with the neighboring clans of Pukë, Lurë, Selitë, Lezhë, and Zadrimë.

Orosh is regarded as the oldest brother, and as the main *bajrak*, even though it has fewer houses than the others. It was there that the *Kapedan* of Mirditë had his residence, and it was he who was the true ruler of the region. Orosh has a total of about 250 houses, Spaç has around 1,000, Dibër around 800, Fan perhaps 500 and Kuzhnen about 300.

---

[3] Tribal custom did not permit marriage between members of the same clan, or even, as in this case, between members of different clans that originated from the same family.

As to the form of government, we could say that Mirditë was an Aristocratic Republic. The governing body was made up of the *Kapedan*, who served as president, five *bajraktars*,[4] five elders, and fifteen alternate elders. Every *bajrak* had a *bajraktar*, an elder, and several alternate elders whose number varied according to the importance of the clan. All of these offices were hereditary, the office going from the father to the oldest son. If it happened that the office holder had no heir, then his oldest brother inherited the office, following his death.

The general meetings were held in the Church of Shpal, or in the gorge of Orosh. They were attended by the twenty-five persons we noted above, and by the *Halia*, a collective body that included "one man per household." The meetings served for the reconciliation of families in blood feud, and decided on questions of war, and on especially important matters pertaining to the *bajraks*. These meetings were presided over by the *Kapedan*, and all decisions taken at the meetings were made public by him. The *Halia* was of great importance, because the decisions taken by the chiefs could not be put into effect if the members of the *Halia*, who were the direct representatives of the people, were opposed to them. The *Kapedan* had the last word on any disagreements, but even his powers were limited.

Local questions were settled by the elders, alternate elders and the *Halia*. For example, if two families in a village quarreled over the borders of a piece of land, a forest ,etc., then each of them called on two old men for the peaceful settlement of the dispute. If the families failed to reach accord, the matter was referred to the elder of the *bajrak* who, together with the four old men ,was authorized to settle the matter. Question of greater importance were referred to the *bajraktar*, or to the *Kapedan* for settlement.

At the conclusion of the trial, the two sides in the dispute would "come forth with money for the elders," in the amount of 200 *grosh* (old Turkish money) per elder.[5] "They awarded them a pair of sandals," as the saying goes, that is to say, the disputing sides gave the

---

[4] The *bajraktar* was the head of the administrative unit, known as *bajrak*.

[5] According to the custom, the two quarreling parties would choose a council of two or more elders to mediate the dispute, for which service they were paid 200 *grosh* apiece in advance.

elders enough money to buy a pair of sandals, as a reward for their trouble.

There was no written law in Mirditë, and justice was implemented on the basis of the Law of Lek Dukagjin.[6] The law of the Lek has been in force for generations. Today the Government of Albania is making efforts to put into effect the new system of laws, but it is difficult to implement fully the new laws in a land where the mentality of the inhabitants is not in accord with them.

According to the current administrative division of Albania, Mirditë is a sub-prefecture, with the headquarters at Repës. It has six communes, and a police force to keep the peace in the region. The police have set up a variety of stations in certain dangerous areas for the purpose of maintaining public order.

During the time of Turkish rule, Mirditë did not pay any taxes, except for 100 *para*[7] per household, which "were written on the gate of Istanbul," presumably because they were so difficult to collect, and once collected deserved public notice. Even today this "blessed" land does not pay any taxes; yet, if necessary, Mirditë is ready to provide the Government with one able-bodied man per house. At the time of our journey in the region, the communes were asking each family to pay a small amount (one or two crowns) to defray the cost of putting new numbers on the houses. But the men of Mirditë were not in the mood to pay. A highlander said to me one day:

"We don't want to pay for it, because it can become a habit."

---

6 Lek Dukagjini was a Medieval Albanian prince from Dukagjin, who formulated the code of unwritten laws which governed tribal life among the Gegs in northern Albania and Albanian-populated areas in present-day Yugoslavia until recent times.

7 Old Turkish currency, equal in value to 1/40 of a *grosh*.

3
Houses

We might say that, wherever possible, villages were built close to water. Because of fear of homicide, caused by conflicts between neighbors who live very close to each other, houses were built far apart, and a man can walk for a long time before he comes to the last house of the village.

I have seen houses on top of rocks, and in such isolated spots that the mind of a man wonders how it is possible for people to live in places with such bad communications. Self-defense and arable land are the two things that determine the choice of site for a home. The question of social intercourse was not taken into consideration, since every house was independent of other houses.

The house of a Mirditë resident is surrounded by a planted field. The house is built of stone, in order to better withstand the ravages of warfare. The windows are small. Over the door there is a small window with several loopholes through which to shoot firearms. In the corners of the house one sees other narrow lockouts, designed to assure protection for the home on all sides. A house of two floors is called a *kullë*. The roof is covered with slabs or tile, but in areas that are close to pine forests, it is covered with planks. Seen from a distance, the houses look like match boxes.

There are also one-story houses of stone or wood, with roofs of tile, planks, slabs or straw. These are the houses of the lowest classes.

Adjacent to the house is a big basket for the corn, one or two haystacks, a hut, and a little garden planted with cabbages or other vegetables.

The *kullë* may have three, four, or five rooms. If there is no adjacent hut, a partition on the ground floor is used to shelter the livestock. This is located just behind the entrance to the house. A narrow stairway leads to the men's chamber, where the guests are received. As soon as you enter, you are face to face with the fireplace. I have found all kinds of designs for chimney fronts, directly above the fireplace: round ones, square, and conical.

I have seen mantelpiece cornices of stone, etc., and hearths of granite and clay. In single-story houses the hearth is in the middle of the room, and lacks a chimney to draw the smoke out. An earthen jug hangs by a chain over the fire. A part of the fireplace is used for stacking firewood. A light fixture made of wire, hangs from the ceiling, and is used to hold the torch which lights the room. All the leftovers from the meals are thrown down a little hole cut out on the floor in front of the fireplace.

The room does not have much furniture. Heavy blankets of goat-hair, or sheepskins, spread out on the floor at each corner of the room. Here and there one sees a few short-legged chairs, a carved antique stool of great beauty, or an old carved chest. You might also notice a block of wood in a corner of the room. It is used as a pillow.

On both sides of the chimney and on the walls there are niches of carved wood. They are beautiful, and are used as cupboards for coffee sets. Near the hearth, close to where the head of the house sits, there is an opening for pouring down the dirty water, after the coffee cups are washed. The waste water makes its way to the barn nearby. Fresh coffee is served the guests at a moment's notice.

As we said above, the windows of the house are small, without panes, and are closed by means of thick, solid shutters. The walls are white-washed and without decorations. However, one might see hanging on the walls a gun (when a permit has been obtained), a *shefteli*,[8] a cross or an icon, or perhaps a photograph of the head of the house, which may have been taken in the city of Shkodër or Tiranë. Slightly below the ceiling, on the wall, may be seen a few iron hooks that were used formerly for hanging the rifles of warriors. Such hooks can also be seen on the outer door of the house.

The ceiling may be constructed of planks, or a type of lattice work. If the fireplace is in the middle of the room, the smoke goes up past beautiful smoke-blackened beams and through the tiled roof.

Salted meats hang from the ceiling, above the hearth. Below the ceiling runs a horizontal bar of wood, on which wet clothes are spread out to dry.

---

[8] A stringed musical instrument, characteristic of northern Albania and other Geg-populated areas. At present, the standard spelling of the instrument is *çifteli*.

There is a water pitcher and trough for washing the hands. One can also wash at the wash basin which is also located within the room. The waste water empties out the house through a little opening.

The toilet, built like a little box against the wall, is on the second floor. Its walls are strong, and it has, in addition, one or two loopholes for shooting firearms. The wastes do not empty into a drain pipe, but rather outside the house, which makes for a nauseating sight.

4

Family Life

The Mirditë family operates under the patriarchal system. The oldest male is the master of the house. He receives guests, he is the first to begin to eat at mealtime, he is the first to speak on any subject, and his word is obeyed without question.

A Mirditë household may have 10, 20, 30 and sometime 40 people. Everyone of them knows his place and respects those who are older than himself.

In a family of many brothers, the oldest brother takes the place of the elder when he dies. Due respect is shown to the mother, who holds the keys to the house, and also has charge of all the daughters-in-law in the house.

There is moreover a hierarchy among the daughters-in-law. The youngest occupies a lower rung the others, and must honor them in the same manner that she honors the old folk.

When the mother dies, the oldest daughter-in-law takes her place.

In large households, the men eat separately, and so do the women and children. The youngest bride pours water for the men to wash their hands, and this chore is considered a privilege. At mealtime the women remain standing, in order to serve the men. Each one in the house must wait for the older ones to start eating before joining them.

In families without sons, the oldest member of the household, be it a man or woman, handles the affairs of the house.

The youngest daughter-in-law is responsible for washing and rubbing the feet of the old men and women, a chore that she considers a privilege.

The men never address their wives by name, and the same goes for other women in the house. What you hear are cries like: "Oh grandmother! Oh woman! Oh bride!" It seems that the Mirditë woman was not born to be honored. They marveled at us upon seeing that we gave the woman in our team coffee and brandy to drink before we had any, and offered her the best place to sit. Such actions were rebellious, from their point of view.

The duties of the wife are manifold. She cooks, cleans the house, looks after the children and the livestock, works in the fields, cuts wood in the mountains and hauls it home, etc. Whereas the husband receives guests, drives the oxen, takes perhaps the livestock to the mountains, and rolls cigarettes all day long.[9] In olden times he also "fingered the trigger" of his firearms. He may, in addition, busy himself with politics!

The Mirditë man pays the father of his wife-to-be the sum of nearly 10-15 "*qesesh*" (the equivalent of 20-30 "*napolona*"),[10] when he marries her. This bad custom has much to do with the attitude the husband takes toward his wife, although this depends to some extent on the individual. He thinks that, since he pays for her, he must work her to the bones. This custom gives the women a feeling of inferiority, since they are obliged to obey blindly their domineering husbands.

What follows is a conversation we had with a peasant woman from Kallmet, which applies point by point also to the highlanders of Mirditë.

We were sitting atop some stones by the brook of Kallmet when we noticed four peasant women coming down from the mountain, with loads of wood on their backs, and knitting sox or spinning wool as they walked.

They stopped for a while, and were curiously eyeing Dr. Coon's wife, who was dressed like a man. I approached one of them, and I asked her:

"Eh, what do you think? Is the person you see here, dressed in pantaloons of goat-skin, a man or a woman?"

The highland woman answered: "She is a woman and she was born on a lucky day."

"But why?" I said to her.

She replied: "Can't you see the load of wood I'm carrying on my back? I have been on the road for six hours. My hands are battered and bruised from cutting wood in the mountain. Look at my hands, then look at the hands of this woman. Look how white hers are! Do

---

9 The men in Mirditë made their own cigarettes by rolling the tobacco in cigarette paper, then lighting it.

10 A *napolon* was worth 20 gold francs; thus, the total sum paid for the bride was 400 to 600 gold francs.

you see me? I'm not more than 26, yet I look much older, because of the heavy work I do."

That is how the hapless sheep spoke, her eyes fixed on the American lady, whose coat she kept rubbing gently.

"But why don't the men go to the mountain to cut wood?" I said to her.

"What," she replied, "let the men go fetch wood? No, my husband paid money for me and expects me to work. If I didn't work, he would say to me that I'm not worth the bread I eat, and at night he would beat me up with a stick."

There was no use continuing the discussion. However untutored they were, these women were able to make comparisons; and seeing how much better off one of their kind was than they made them feel inferior, and I believe heart-broken as well. They were not asleep, but simply condemned to accept the fate that had produced that social condition. To be sure, the men's position is not any better. But yet, certain small differentiations, certain social distinctions place the women on an inferior scale. They know this and feel it, and their hearts are crushed as a result.

5
The Women

The Mirditë woman is brave in every sense of the word. The biggest load of the house falls on her, and she must bear under it without groaning. Nor is that all. She must face up to the great poverty that confronts her every day.

She is like a man, for she does work that requires the strength and energy of a man. She goes to the mountain, cuts wood and fetches it on her back, works in the fields, looks after the livestock, makes all the dairy foods, and keeps house. She is a hard worker. Even when she is walking with a load on her back, or grazing the livestock, she is busy knitting sox or spinning wool. She is far neater than her husband, and her costume is much more "unique" than his. She is frank and articulate, good-looking, and carries herself better than her husband, even though she works harder than he does.

The women's clothing is quite beautiful and may be better appreciated by looking at the photographs in this book. The kerchief she wears on her head, which is called "*facoletë*," is worn above the ears by married women, whereas maidens tuck it under the chin. Around the waist they wear a red embroidered kerchief, and a red tasseled waistband. Unlike married women, however, maidens wear a black waistband. Attached to the belt is a wooden key holder, from which hang all the keys to the house. A long white shirt covers a portion of the long-sleeved vest, and takes on a baggy shape above the sandals. The shirt is covered over by a long, white, sleeveless woolen garment, attractively decorated over the shoulders and the back, along the seams of the garment.

The black, short-sleeved woolen jacket resembles that of the men, and is worn over the sleeveless garment. The chest is adorned with ornaments, such as a necklace of five crowns strung on a silver watch chain. A similar chain bearing a small cross might also adorn the neck. The women's thick fingers are covered with three or four silver rings, whose beauty depends on the taste of the owner. The ears are not ignored either. From them hang silver earrings of different forms, size and style, depending on the bearer. The feet are adorned with leather sandals and lovely sox, which they call "*shputa*" (sneaker socks).

I noticed that the women, even elderly ones, had very dark hair, and shiny too. Perhaps this was due to some dye they used, but I did not have the chance to verify it.

As a sign of mourning for someone who has died, the women cut their hair up front.

6
The Mirditë Man

Before visiting a place, a man has certain ideas about it which may contradict reality. For example, what does the reader think of when he hears the word "highlander"? Does he not imagine a man of huge stature, brave, of ruddy complexion, and many other things of this nature? This is the idea I had, too, about the Mirditë highlander, before visiting his habitat. But that is not the case.

The average Mirditë man is of medium size, long-faced, and wears a mustache. (By God, they say, a man is not a man who does not wear a long mustache!) He has a thin nose, chestnut-color hair and eyes (we have however seen a large number of blue-eyed men), a thin waist, and in general a lanky figure.

Furthermore, he is smart—he catches on quickly—has a smiling face, even though he lives a wretched life, likes to joke, is talkative and speaks rapidly. He is also proud, fanatic—though not in a religious sense—a good warrior and very nimble-footed. Still, he differs from one district to another.

Because of the pervasive poverty, I did not see any Mirditë man who was well dressed, or who wore his native costume complete. Among articles of clothing worn by men, I saw Italian, American, and Austrian army jackets, dating from the time of the Prince,[11] etc. The market of Shkodër is astonishing, because it fills Mirditë with all kinds of cheap clothing.

The standard costume of the Mirditë man is composed of the following parts: black jacket; black or white close-fitting trousers of thick felt, with decorative black ribbons around the pockets, in front, in the back and along the sides; gold-embroidered vest; shirts of different colors; striped-belt; multi-colored sox and thin leather sandals. The cap could be like that worn by the inhabitants of Krujë and Dibër;

[11] The reference is to Prince Wilhelm Wied, the Prussian army captain who ruled Albania for six months (March-September) in 1914.

that is to say curved on top, or flat like a flat-bottomed bowl. The chest may be adorned with a silver chain attached to an antique watch; an engraved pistol; a silver pipe; a cross on a silver chain; and a few silver buttons. Arrayed in this interesting outfit, the Mirditë man strikes a serious pose. The above attire however is worn only by the well-to-do. The needy ones go around in baggy pants made of flax, instead of the white woolen trousers trimmed with black ribbons. In addition, they wear a long white shirt. Otherwise, their costume is the same as that of the well-to-do, except that it lacks polish.

7
The Mirditë Hospitality

Blessed be those feasts with simple plenty crowned,
Where all the ruddy family around
Laugh at the jests or pranks, that never fail,
Or sigh with pity at some mournful tale,
Or press the bashful stranger to his food,
And learn the luxury of doing good.

Goldsmith

The virtue of hospitality, of which we Albanians are proud, but which is gradually disappearing in the cities, has strong foundations in Mirditë.

Whether it is because of their primitive social organization, or the absence of inns and hotels, or the low mobility of the population owing to bad roads, the fact remains that the guest will find an open door everywhere in this region, where he is greeted with the words: "Welcome, oh friends! God has brought you here, oh friend!"

It is the universal custom here; hence, the oft-heard phrase: "It is an honorable house. They receive guests well there."

The house that fails to honor the guest is looked upon with scorn.

For the Mirditë people, receiving guests is a give and take affair, for a man who honors a guest at his home, is in turn honored by the guest when he happens to be in his locality.

Hospitality is not confined to the members of the clan, who may, after all, some day return the courtesy. It is extended to strangers as well. The natives here go even to the extreme of receiving under their roof a man with whom they are in blood feud. Not only do they give him food and drink and shelter; they also offer him protection.

"He has broken bread with me," says the highlander, and therefore he will not harm him and violate the ancient law. If someone should harm the guest who has broken bread in an honorable house, that person is responsible to the master of the house, because by abusing his guest he has dishonored his host as well.

The natives of Mirditë—like Albanians in general—are proud and like to be honored and to honor others. One often hears a highlander here say: The house of such and such has done me great honor. He attaches importance to the place he is given to sit, pays attention to what is said to him, notices the sort of food he is served, and the place where he is to sleep. In other words, he is quite sensitive about matters concerning honor.

In Mirditë, the word "guest" is held in the highest regard. No matter how poor a family may be, it will honor a guest as much as it is able to, and feels sad when it lacks the means to do more for his comfort.

One night in Ungrej I visited a family in a single-story house, that was so poor it broke your heart. We sat around the fire in the middle of the room. The smoke from the lighted torch and the fire were choking us. There was no coffee in the house, as they could not afford it, and our hosts were conscious of this and felt sad. Yet, these lacks did not detract from the hospitality shown us. The old woman of the house took out an apple from a trunk and gave it to me, saying: "Take this apple; I have nothing else to give you."

The importance of the guest in Mirditë is proved also by the fact that if he is killed, his blood can never be compensated for, nor can the matter be settled by the governmental authorities. The matter is instead left into the hands of his host, and the house of the host will not have washed off the mark of disgrace put on it until it takes revenge.

8
Bravery

The Mirditë man—and the highlander in general—is brave, because his eyes has seen many things that call for courage. He is not fearful at all. He is face to face with many situations which contribute to the strengthening of this virtue: wild beasts, crossing rivers on foot, heavy snowfalls, fierce rainstorms, walking alone in dense woods and losing his way, sleeping outdoors at night, engaging in armed battles with enemies, etc. I have enumerated only a few of the hazards, but I believe they suffice to instill terror into the heart of the city dweller, who lives a comfortable life within the city and has no desire to embark on such dangerous adventures.

We must not forget also that poverty makes a man brave. Does it not take a lot of courage to go and grab someone's cow, or ox or goat, when you know that it could cost you your life? Yet, our friend ignores the danger, and makes off with the property of other people. It is because he has been brave—and still is—that in olden times he was hired as a mercenary. But the meager pay he was given in no way compensated for the risks he took.

Raised in these circumstances, the Mirditë man has always been ready to defend his freedom, his honor, and the rights he inherited from his ancestors. Moreover, if someone offended him, he took the matter into his own hands, rather than let another person settle it. Although at present the Government tries to mediate the disputes that arise among them, still they are not satisfied with the solutions arrived at by Governmental authorities, even when such solutions may be just.

The beauty of valor is best expressed in popular songs, which are the mirror of the highlander's soul. Here are some typical lines:

I am a Mirditë man; I don't surrender.
My ancestor, a terrible sword, he;
A mandate he has left us:
Never give up the ancient arms.
....

When he fired the last bullet,
Then only did Gjini fall.

Can anyone envision a more beautiful tableau of valor? The brave highlander preferred to die with honor, rather than violate the tradition of the land, and be called a woman, and be scorned by everyone.

Here is how some other dragon-like men in this region talk: "I will not be taken alive! I will not give up my gun as long as I breathe!"

It is difficult to give up the gun in a land where "the gun crackles like thunder!," where "they fire their rifles from one hilltop to another!," and where "they do battle as custom dictates, to honor themselves and their kin!"

Notice how these lion-hearted men speak when they are insulted:

I have not borne dishonor since the day I was born.
I have never brought shame upon my house,
And my pistol will prove it to you right now!

Another dragon-like highlander, unmindful of the fact that he was dying, says to his comrades:

Tell my mother not to weep for me,
But for my gun that failed to fire!

Another brave one left the following mandate to his comrades, when he saw that he was dying:

Say to my mother that her son got married,
And if, oh Lord, she asks what bride he took.
Say, three bullets in the chest he took!

He took as his bride three bullets in the chest! That is bravery, genuine bravery!

The foregoing speaks above all of individual bravery. But we should not suppose that Mirditë collectively is any less brave. Fighting against her neighbors over some disagreements she has had with them, Mirditë "has not dishonored her own clan." That is why you hear it said around here:

I am the renowned Mirditë,
Renowned for the battle I fought,
When surrounded by three hundred rifles!

Here is another one:

Come Mirditë, in the name of the Lord,
Fight on as tradition calls!

To its neighbor, Lurë, Mirditë talks in this manner:

Where are you, sandal-footed Lurë,
You do not know the red Mirditë,
This Mirditë, people say,
Can dig your grave on the broad mountain terraces.

A highlander said to me one day: "If they take the gun away from us, it's 'goodbye' to valor." Another one complained to me, saying: "They've taken our arms and turned us into old women."

In Mirditë both young and old know the use of firearms. The gun has been their inseparable companion. I believe that even today, regardless of the firearms the Government has collected, the highlanders have at least one rifle hidden away some place, for use when the time calls for it. They could not take their eyes off the long rifle and revolver that the Americans carried with them. And could not rest until they took the firearms in their hands and examined them. They have a lengthy vocabulary in Mirditë about guns. Here are some of the words used: "hutë" (rifle), "*alltije*" (revolver), "*pushk magjare*" (Hungarian rifle), "*karajfile*"* (a type of flint-cock gun made in Italy by the firm Carrari & Figli, whose name was distorted into karajfile—translator's note), "*pushk e gjatë*" (long rifle), "*nagane*" (a type of six-chambered revolver), "*dallap*" (a type of revolver), "*shejshane*," "*mazere*" (Mauser), "*martinë*" (Martin), "*pushkë llatine*" (Latin rifle),

---

* Rifle—from that the distorted name karajfile.

etc. How can a Mirditë inhabitant help but become an expert on guns, when he has a chance to use so many of them!

As we walked along the road, the police would point out to us the places where someone was killed. Here is where they ambushed such and such, the good man would say to me. But that manner of doing away with one's enemy left me with misgivings about the meaning of true bravery. It is not an act of bravery to find a hidden spot, and from there to shoot your enemy, without giving him a chance to fight back like a man. To lay ambush is mean, and men who are truly brave will not stoop to such a practice. The people of Mirditë think that ambush is dishonorable. They admire instead the man who says:

"It is I, Mark, and I meet you face to face!"

The truly brave man says: "Wait for me, I'm coming!"

And the other answers: "Come, I'm waiting!"

The guns fire, and down goes he whose time is up. Another man might address his "enemy" in these words:

> Why didn't you step out into the open,
> So that the muzzles of our guns might
> exchange their fiery kiss!

9

Greetings and Oaths

In Mirditë it is not enough to merely shake hands when greeting someone. One must solemnly touch both temples of the other's head. This is also the way two men, or a man and a woman greet each other, when they meet after a certain length of time.

They accompany these actions with words such as the following: "How are you, man? Long life to you. Are you able? Are you tired?"

The replies vary. For example: "Are you in sound health? May you enjoy good health. Getting there slowly, little by little."

The women greet each other this way: " How are you?"

And the answer is: "May you live with honor; and may we have you in our midst. How are you?"

When they drink whiskey: "Glory be to Christ; to our honor; I'm glad I find you well; I greet you; may good come to you; cheers."

The replies are: "For as long as you live; may you live with honor; I welcome you; may he who sees you greet you with honor; may it do you good; may I welcome you time and again; may you be around for a long time."

He who hands a glass of whiskey over to another says, "*Tungjatjeta*," meaning "I greet you," (literally, "A long life to you"), and the other replies in kind.

At weddings: "To a lucky wedding; may the Lord bless it."

And the other replies: "May you prosper and be lucky."

When a baby is born: "May the baby have a long life."

To which the other replies: "Bless your tongue."

When someone dies: "May the Lord give you strength; it is good that you are well."

And the reply: "May you be honored for the courtesy of your visit; may you enjoy good health, along with your friends and your relatives."

As the visitors leave the home of the deceased, they say: "May we never come here again in sorrow."

The others reply: "May Christ receive him in Paradise."

On holidays: "May you enjoy good times ahead."

And the reply: "May all of us be in good health."

The Mirditë people swear as follows: "By heaven and earth; in the name of the great God; by the image of God; by that fire; by the cross of Christ; by that church; by the head of my sons," etc.

10

Kreshtë-Rrapës

Around noon, we left the Kallmet village in Zadrimë, and headed for Mirditë. We started off on an uphill at a leisurely pace, and after a few hours reached the peak of the Kreshtë pass. Behind us lay a most beautiful panorama: The sun shone on the plain of Zadrimë, and the Drin river, winding its way like a serpent, sparkled in the sunlight. Far off in the direction of Shkodër could be seen, but just barely, the mountain of Tarabosh, whose top was covered by white clouds. The beauty of the scene was enhanced by big and little hills of varied hues. Not far from the pass was the Peak of Veljë, which was covered with patches of snow. There is a legend about this peak, whose name means "sail." It says that in olden times, when all the surrounding land was under water, the peak served to anchor with chains all the sail-boats in the area.

A hut at the pass marked the location of the police station. As soon as we arrived there, we were met by a policeman who greeted us, saying: "How are you? Did you get on well? Are you tired?"

He shook hands politely with Prof. Coon and his wife, but gave me the traditional highland reception. He clasped my hand, put his left hand on my shoulder, then touched both temples of my head with his, while at the same time repeating the standard formula for the welcome. It was our first exposure to the Mirditë way of welcome.

Feeling tired, we sat down on some rocks and rested for about ten minutes. The policeman took out his tobacco box and offered us some for a smoke. We for our part gave him a few ready-made cigarettes.

At this point we changed police, replacing the one from Kallmet with another officer. This one was from Mirditë, a pleasant and quick man named Simon. With him leading the way, we set off for Ungrej, where we were to stay for several days. Along the way Simon talked to me about the customs of the land.

Our path followed closely the water of Dibri. As we trekked along, we left behind us mountains and hills that had a melancholy look. After a few hours we reached the village of Fregnë. We then continued our journey to Ungrej, where we arrived quite late.

Simon led us directly to the Inn of Ungrej. As soon as we got there, the owner of the inn came out to welcome us.

"*Urdhnoni! Urdhnoni*!" (come in, come in!), he said. He ushered us into a ground-floor room, warmed by a blazing fire. The fireplace was in the middle of the room, and all around it on the floor lay boards for lodgers to sleep on. A jug was steaming over the fire, and salted meat hung from the ceiling.

Being tired, we sat down to rest, while Mark,[12] who had lived in Shkodër for a considerable time, brought *raki*[13] and *meze*.[14] While partaking of these around the blazing fire, I noticed that someone was sticking his head inside our room from time to time, for a look at these "amazing visitors."

The Inn at Ungrej has a sleeping room, which Mark prepared carefully for us. There was a bed in it! The table was covered with a table-cloth, and on it the clever fellow had placed apples and shelled walnuts. All this gave the table a nice appearance.

Let us not forget that we were in Mirditë!—the land of bears, and knee-deep snow! And nothing to eat! How different was the reality! Mark served us some broiled meat, as well as a dish of stewed meat. We ate everything with great gusto. All the apples and walnuts we could wish were there for the taking. Mark's place was the best in Ungrej. The first night we ate Albanian style, sitting on the floor by the fireplace. We ate with wooden spoons.

We were awakened early in the morning by the crow of an angry rooster. Besides the rooster, there was the coughing of our old mule driver, who merits a brief description: He was a man of short stature and broad shoulders. His hands were full of sores, the result—he told us later—of kicks that his horse had dealt him. He had a dark complexion, an unshaved beard, and he went about with his pants unbuttoned. He had a "vague" look on his face that somehow aroused

---

[12] Presumably the name of the proprietor of the inn.

[13] *Raki* is a clear brandy, made of grapes or plums, and traditionally the most popular alcoholic beverage in the country.

[14] The appetizers consisted invariably of feta cheese and olives, but sometimes sliced eggs or other food items were served as well.

fear. He was an ill-tempered man from Zadrimë, and his name was Zef.

We spent several days in Ungrej. While there, Prof. Coon made measurements of the men in the locality. In the meantime Mark took better care of us with each passing day, so that we did not feel we were in rugged Mirditë at all. For a time he even brought us beer from Lezhë to drink.

"You must come and be measured!" That was the order given by the head of the Ungrej commune to the elders roundabout. But these words meant nothing to them. Be measured? But why? Who wanted these measurements? The Government? And if so, why? For army recruitments? Taxes? Labor? It was with misgivings that these men came to be measured, some of whom consulted with one another before going through with it.

"Please come, please come!" the good man said to us, his eyes sparkling with joy.

On the following day we left for Rras, which we reached in about an hour, after traveling through hills clothed with lovely oak, groves.

In Rras, a woman was standing at the front door of her house, and watching us with curiosity as we passed by. A boy from Mirditë in our party shouted at her:

"Oh, woman, go and tell your husband to come out and be measured!"

The simple woman answered: "What for? I've already measured him myself!"

Our friend in Rras was waiting for us, and as soon as we arrived at his home—which stood on a hill near the village brook—he came over and shook hand with us, and said with all his heart:

"*Oshxheldën! Oshxheldën*!" (A Turkish greeting meaning "Welcome!"—translator's note). He greeted me according to the Albanian tradition, while with the Americans he simply shook hands.

He then led us up a wooden staircase to the men's parlor, where he had lit a big fire. Quickly, he offered a carved seat to Mrs. Coon, and seated her at the place of honor.[15] He gave to each of the rest of us a stool to sit on, after which we drew close to the fireplace. Our

---

15 Presumably she was placed on the right side of the hearth, since this was regarded as the most prestigious place in the room.

host sat on the floor to the left of the fireplace, with his legs crossed. At this point the ritual of the welcome began, as our beaming host asked us, one by one, "How are you? Are you holding up well? Are you tired?"[16] Prof. Coon and his wife had learned a few Albanian words, and replied:

"*Mirë, falemneries! falemneries*!" (Fine, thank you, thank you!)

Our host took out his tobacco box, and rolled a cigarette for each of us to light up. Then he began to make coffee for us. The coffee roaster was over a niche near the mantelpiece. He reached over and brought it down, and put in it a handful of coffee beans. He turned the roaster carefully over the fire, as he continued to talk to us. After a few minutes the coffee was roasted. Next, he ground it in a mill made in Europe.[17] When the coffee was brewed, he poured it into a pitcher so as to strain it. In short, he made it just as they do in Europe. He washed the cups, poured the coffee, placed a bit of sugar in each cup, stirred it well, then gave us to drink, while placing the hand over his heart.[18]

We had about four rounds of coffee, and we could have had more if we wanted.

Soon the room was filled with men who sat cross-legged on the floor, and with children from the village and from our host's own household. Women, too, came in and circled all around us, some carrying infants in their arms, and others holding them by the hand. All of them marveled at us, especially at Prof. Coon's wife, who was dressed in men's clothes.

At the time, our host's sister, a bride of four months, had come to visit him. Thrilled with Prof. Coon's wife, she stood by her side and every now and then kissed her hand. A few of the older children sat close to us, and one of them, a boy, about ten years old, massaged the hands of the guests from joy.

---

16 The custom in Albania required the host, as a matter of courtesy, to address each of the guests with the same stock phrases of welcome.

17 The reference here is to the more advanced countries of Western Europe, since Albania of course is also Europe.

18 This was a customary gesture of affection and respect in the highlands toward the guest.

The time came to go outside to measure the men who had assembled there. This job continued for approximately two hours, and was carried out amid laughter and jokes. The men did not know the purpose of the measurements, and made fun of whoever was about to be measured. They would say to one, "It's to fetch you a bride from America;" to another, "It's to fit you out in a red suit;" and to still another, "The gentleman from America is about to bless you so that you will be immune to malaria." And so it went. This good-humored teasing caused all who were present to split their sides laughing. The jesters in the village became special targets of this teasing.

When we finished our work, we went back to the house for lunch. The table was set, and the *nuse* (bride)[19] brought us a wash basin [20] and a pitcher of water with which to wash our hands. In the meantime, our host came over with some cheese on a plate, and a jug of *raki*, and proceeded to pour us all a drink. It was grape brandy, but not very strong.

"Welcome! Welcome!" the good man toasted us, and Prof. and Mrs. Coon answered with, "*Falemneries, falemneries*!"

"I salute you. May you grow in honor!" our good friend went on with his toast. The Mirditë man in our party replied:

"May you be honored by all men you meet. May you be my guest!" etc.

We livened up after drinking the entire jug of brandy. Lunch was served, beginning with soup that came in an earthen pot. We ate with wooden spoons, and from the same bowl. The head of the house cut a loaf of corn bread, and began to eat, after crossing himself and saying slowly, "In the name of the Father, the Son, and the Holy Spirit."

The soup was followed by stewed chicken, which we finished off quickly. We were satiated at this point. But in spite of that, they brought us some *petulla* (balls of batter fried in oil) to eat as well. But since our bellies were full, we almost got sick at the sight of them. Yet, we had to eat them, in order not to offend our host. The Americans and I exchanged glances, then gulped down a few of them,

---

19 The term *nuse* or bride was used to refer not only to a newly-married woman, but generally to the daughter-in-law in the house, especially the youngest one, if there were several of them under one roof.

20 This was actually a hollowed out chunk of wood, or a kind of trough.

dipped in honey. Our host urged us to go on eating. We declined politely, and finished the repast by drinking a glass of thin, red wine that they had made themselves. Apparently, the wine was not of good vintage, as it was not fit to drink. But again, we had to drink it!

At the end of meal, they again brought us water to wash the hands, removed the *sofër*[21] and swept the floor thoroughly. We then moved close to the fireplace. Our host ordered the children to go to another room to eat lunch. To the other men who happened to be in the room he said: "You are welcome to sit down and share the food the Lord has given us."

They answered: "May you grow in honor, but we have already eaten."

Again they served us coffee, and rolled cigarettes for us. Shortly after, the children returned and sat down by the fireplace. The head of the house reached for the çifteli, and sang a few songs of valor. He played the two stringed instrument well, and with great dexterity.

We had an interesting discussion with those present, and noted that they suffered from feelings of inferiority.

"Our country is poor," they said. "The soil is bad, and lacks irrigation. The roads are bad, the children have no schooling, and the population is ignorant."

It was getting late, as we had to return to Ungrej. So we begged our host to give us permission to leave.

"Stay for the night," his sister said to us, and our host and the children said the same thing. "Stay over, it will be such fun," they all said.

"*Falemneries, falemneries*," replied Prof. Coon and his wife, as we prepared to depart.

We stepped out into the yard, and there the Americans took a photograph of the entire family of our host. This pleased them a lot, especially when we promised that we would send them a copy of the photo.

Noting the long rifle that Prof. Coon carried with him, our host could not rest until he took it in his hands and examined it carefully. Then he requested that I ask Prof. Coon for permission to fire it once.

---

21 The *sofër* was a round table, about a foot high, which was set on the floor at meal time, then was put away to clear the floor.

Coon agreed gladly. The highlander took aim at a white stone that was perhaps 200 or more meters away. Bang! He fired, and shattered the stone to pieces. Prof. Coon was amazed.

After this ceremony, we took our leave of the women in the house, gave each of the children a coin, and went away with the best of memories.

As is the custom in Mirditë, our host accompanied us to a considerable distance down the road. Furthermore, seeing that we still had to cross the river bed of Rras, he ordered the boys who had come along with him to carry us across the bed on their backs.

We said goodbye at this point to this noble man, crossed the stream, and headed back to Ungrej at a leisurely pace. Along the way we spoke of nothing but the fine reception we had a Rras.

On and on we traveled, and now twilight was begging to fall. The policeman with our party proposed that we spend the night over at the house of the elder of Kalivaç, which lay on the way. After a while we came to the house, and the policeman struck the front door and yelled: "Oh, woman, where is the old man?"

A woman came out to the door, with a cigarette in her mouth. She looked around suspiciously, then said to the policeman: "My husband is not home. He went to Shkodër."

The truth is that the man had not gone to Shkodër, but was hiding inside. He came out later. His behavior made a bad impression on the natives who heard the incident, because truly the friendly welcome is the established custom in the region.

We left Kalivaç, and within an hour arrived at the Inn of Ungrej, where Mark had prepared an abundant table for us: stewed chicken, apples, shelled walnuts, beer, etc. We really stuffed ourselves at dinner, after which Prof. Coon and his wife retired for the night.

The small room with the fireplace was filled with people. The jug of *raki* made its rounds, our policeman played the çifteli, another man sang, others laughed and made conversations, while Mark saw to it that everyone enjoyed himself. The hours of the evening passed by with song, anecdotes, and fables. I went to sleep very late, and very tired.

We finished our work in Ungrej, and early in the morning on the following day set off for Simon, a village in the *bajrak* of Kuzhnen. Being very pleased with our visit, Mark let us have his best mule for the journey ahead, and in addition arranged for the boy who worked in his store to accompany us.

With the policeman leading our party, we made our way through the plain of Papërdhak, crossed the stream of Ungrej, passed Çavorë and finally reached Simon. Once there, we went straight to the communal office, where we were met by a short, round-faced, agile young man. He was the head of the commune, and he lost no time in instructing his aides to find lodging for us. In the meantime, we waited in the office of the young man, which served him also as a bedroom. Both fresh and salted meat hung from the ceiling above the steps leading to his office-bedroom. The poor fellow apologized to us for the condition of his room, because it lacked any appeal!

An old man came over to take us to his house atop of the hill. The horses forded the stream that lay on the way, while we crossed it by treading on a log that had served as a bridge over the stream. As we struggled up the hill, one of our horses tumbled down, causing Zef to burst out swearing in his usual manner.

At last we reached the home of the old man, who ushered us into the men's parlor. A woman swept the floor, and afterward they gave us each a blanket to sit on. The fire was burning brightly, and the head of the house brought in still more brushwood. Being awfully grimy from the trip, we needed a good scrubbing. So we heated up a lot of water over the fireplace, then cleaned up.

In this house, too, the parlor was filled with men from the village, who looked at us with curiosity. Then, a man came in with some cutlets for us from the head of the commune. Prof. Coon took the meat and, employing all the skill of a butcher, cut it into thin slices. Next, he rolled the slices nicely, and got ready to broil them. At this point, one of two skinny black cats that were circling about us, grabbed a good chunk of the meat and took off. Our host, however, dashed after the cat and took the meat right out of its mouth. He also brought in some pork meat, which the women broiled for us in their own quarters. We prepared the cutlets ourselves; only it turned out that they were tough as leather. It was billy goat meat! Just the same, we sat down to dinner and ate everything. Here we used our own china—plates, etc.—and everyone was amazed at these West European products. Their amazement reached the zenith when they saw Mrs. Coon sleep in a tarpaulin-type sac.

Prof. Coon and his wife slept in one corner of the room, while the rest of us and the head of the house slept in another corner. We lay down on boards, using a log for a pillow. The cutlets did a job on me; I was not able to sleep a wink all night long because of indigestion. Besides, our peace and quiet was broken by the mice that scampered about the beams on the ceiling, and the cats that were rummaging through our belongings.

We were up early in the morning. The men began to arrive to be measured. While being measured they teased one another in the same manner that we noted previously. We took the measurements of the head of the commune, as well, as he would have been disappointed if we did not include him. When we completed our quota, we took a few photographs, then began to get ready to depart.

As Zef and some other men loaded up the horses, Prof. Coon handed me a few crowns to give to our host for his children. After the other members of our party bid him goodbye, I pressed the crowns on his hand as a modest token of our appreciation of his hospitality.

"For all the trouble I went to in your behalf, even if you gave me 70 crowns, it would not be enough," our host said to me.

I felt as if the roof fell over my head when I heard these words from the mouth of a Mirditë man. To think we are a country renowned for its hospitality! I said to myself: They have begun to destroy those beautiful customs of which Albanians are so proud. The spirit of commercialism has begun to creep even here. But perhaps our host reacted that way because previous visitors had taken unfair advantage of him, owing to the fact that his house lay right by the road, and was the most accessible as well as the best house in Simon. The biggest difficulty a traveler faces in Mirditë is that he cannot discuss prices there. The host honors you with his welcome as a matter of course, and in turn feels greatly honored when you, as a guest, give something to his children.

Upon leaving this mercenary place, we crossed the stream of Simon, and headed for the pass of Valmer. We crossed the bridge of the Fan at the big ford, climbed the great gradient of Shpal and finally arrived at the church of Shpal,[22] renowned as the conference site of

---

22 *Shpal* appears to be a contraction of the words *Shën Pal* (previously *Shënjt Pal*), meaning "St. Paul."

the representatives of the five *bajraks*. The church has been built on an open space that is not too wide, but which is surrounded by beautiful landscape. The sun was setting now, giving the gorge across, half-bathed in its light, a majestic look. Leaving the church, we traveled downhill toward Blinisht, where we encountered another striking panorama. Here and there and on top of the hills you see houses that look like Medieval castles. Mountains! Wherever you look you see mountains.

Who can describe the feelings experienced here by the soul that has left behind the dust and noise of the city, and has come to this quiet place, where one hears only the tinkling of a bell worn by a prized ram, the sound of a distant flute, and the slow and steady echo of a limpid stream, whose source is far, far away in the lofty mountains covered with snow! The tranquil sight of range upon range of countless mountains enchants the eye, and the soul of man falls into a slumber of sweet dreams that brings it into affinity with the spirit of the mountains. And that spirit, in turn, caressing the soul fraternally, leads it to fountainheads of heavenly beauty, where for a brief while it can quench its great thirst for beauty.

As the poet Thomson[23] wrote:

> Thrice happy he! who on the sunless side
> Of a romantic mountain, forest crown'd,
> Beneath the whole collected shade reclines;
> Or in the gelid caverns, wood pine wrought,
> And fresh bedew'd with ever spouting streams,
> Sits coolly calm; while all the world without
> Unsatisfy'd, and sick tosses at noon.

Musing on these lines, we came to the village of Blinisht. The policeman wanted to take us to a big house on top of a knoll, which resembled an ancient fortress. On a field near the house, he met the owner, an old man, and asked him to provide quarters for our party. We had no luck, however, as the old man had a group of thirty prisoners in the house that night, so there was no place left for us.

---

23 The reference is probably to the Scottish poet, James Thomson (1700-1748) author of *The Seasons*, a poem of delicate feeling for nature.

Nevertheless, he said to the officer that we were welcome to stay, if we wished, but feared that we would be "most uncomfortable." This caused us to go to another house a little farther.

Walking ahead of us, our policeman approached a little girl outside her house, and asked her: "Where are the men of the house, little girl?"

Frightened, the poor girl replied: "They're over in the mountain, so help me God!"

She then called out to her grandmother, who came out to see what was happening.

With Prof. and Mrs. Coon off at a distance, I decided to walk over to the girl, who seemed to be about ten, and in a friendly voice, unlike that of the policeman, asked her: "Where are the men, little girl?"

"They're over in the mountain, so help me God!" she repeated.

"Do not be afraid," I said to her. "We are not evil people. We have an American woman with us, and you should see how nice she is! But night has fallen on us, and we are looking for a place to sleep,"

This time she asked me: "What does the policeman want with the men? Does he want to put them in prison?"

"No," I said, "he wants to talk to them about getting a place for us, because we're strangers here."

After being reassured, the poor girl said to me with all her heart: "I welcome you, whom God has brought here!"

She was quite pleased when I told her to come and meet the very kind American lady.

I called Prof. and Mrs. Coon and the mule drivers to come on over, because the mistress of the house was pleased to receive us in her home. The caravan arrived, and an old woman of about seventy took our hand and said, "Welcome!" Then she led us to the guest room, which was warmed by the fireplace, and in the other corner she placed Mrs. Coon. Now began the ceremony of greetings: "How are you? How are you getting along? Are you tired?," etc.

Although our hostess was along in years, she had the energy of a young woman. From her corner she gave orders to the young daughters-in-law, who obeyed her at once. Her only son had been killed accidentally at the time of the Austrian occupation,[24] leaving the hapless woman to bear the burden of the house herself, like a man. The house was more or less well off. It had a good-sized meadow round about, plus a little bit of land for planting. She had a grandson living with her, but she said that a grandchild is not the same as your own son.

We made ourselves comfortable, and afterward began to chat.

"By Heaven," the old woman said to me, "if somebody comes to my door, I cannot let him die outside my home!"

These and other things spoke the good woman, in a strong and imposing voice. In the meantime, the daughters-in-law remained on their feet, the little girl we spoke of above stood close by Mrs. Coon, smiling all the time, while the old woman's grandchildren, whom she could not enjoy, crowded around her.

In a few minutes her nephew—the man of the house—arrived from the mountains, and sat in the old woman's place. We then persuaded her to take the second spot, namely, Mrs. Coon's place. She accepted reluctantly, however, because it was not their custom, she said, to sit in the guest's place.

The man now took out his tobacco box, and offered us some for a light. At the same time he began to make coffee for us. But it was served without sugar, since there was none in the house, and the nearest store was very far from Blinisht. Mrs. Coon proposed to her husband that we give our hosts a good measure of sugar from our own provisions. Prof. Coon agreed. I then asked the old woman to bring over a container, and she was very pleased when we filled it to the brim.

"Now the old woman has plenty of sugar for her coffee, " she said.

When we finished drinking coffee, she told the *nuses* to bring the *raki*, along with some feta cheese. We drank as much of the *raki* as we could, then opened a bottle of our cognac. We passed it around among the women and the older children. But the women were bashful and hesitated to drink. They had never tried it before, and you should have seen the faces they made when they emptied a glass! But when we

---

24 The time referred to is World War I, when the Austrian army occupied a large part of Albania.

told the old woman that it was good for the health, she downed another glass!

Finally, one of the *nuses* brought over the wash basin and a pitcher of water, so we could wash our hands. It was the signal for dinner. In fact, our hostess told one of the women to set the table, and another to serve the food. They bought us a big loaf of corn bread and broiled pork meat, which we ate with great relish. We filled ourselves up, then thanked the lady of the house for the treat. The dining table was now put away, the floor was swept, and we again gathered around the fireplace. Our host began to make us another cup of coffee. We smoked many rounds of cigarettes, and seeing that the old woman smoked, too, we gave her a pack of cigarettes. She could not thank us enough for it. "May you grow in honor," she kept saying, etc.

The *nuses* at this point went downstairs to eat dinner, after getting the cue from the old woman. Soon, the children also disappeared, as they, too, went downstairs to eat.

In the meantime, our hostess was asking Mrs. Coon: How long had she been married? How many children did she have? Did she miss the loved ones she had left behind in America? How far was America from Mirditë? Did America have mountains like Mirditë?, etc. When Mrs. Coon showed her a paragraph of her son, the old woman asked how could she leave him alone! Did she have any feelings for the child? Then she gave Mrs. Coon an apple for her son in America.

The children returned and drew close to the fire. In our belongings we had a large catalogue of costumes, similar to "*Bon Marché*,"[25] which I took out to show to the children. It contained colored illustrations of children's clothing, and made the greatest impression on the children, as well as on the women, who looked at it with great curiosity. I cut out a few of the figures to give to them, and they held on to those as if they were church icons. They marveled at the works of America!

Then we played "cups," a kind of party game. A little boy beat me at "*spathish*"—a type of card game in which the jack can pick up all the cards on the table.

---

25 It is not clear to what the author is referring here. He might be talking about a French magazine of the time.

While we laughed and played games near the hearth, in the back of the room, an elderly woman kept popping up her head from behind some trunks. With her pale face and cavernous eyes, she struck fear in you. Was she demented! "Look behind you," the American lady, who had noticed her already, said to me. Yet when the time came to go to bed, some of the children went to sleep with the woman, and this gave me to understand that she was not demented. But why didn't she come out to meet us, as did the other women? I don't know what to say; but she was fearful to look at.

It was time to go to sleep. Prof. and Mrs. Coon got into their sleeping bags. As for me, our host spread out a few sheepskins and some straw on the floor, then covered me up with a blanket of goat's hair. I lay down with my clothes on. We were very tired, and I should have fallen asleep right away. But I could not, because of what my eyes had seen earlier. It was very late in the night when I fell asleep.

Dawn came, and we got up hurriedly, as we had a long journey ahead of us. Our destination was the house of the *Kapedan* in Orosh. The horses were loaded, and after we took our leave of everyone in the house and gave money presents to the kids, we started on the road to Orosh.

We recrossed the bridge of the Fan, and came to the sub-prefecture of Rrepës. There we met the sub-prefect, who received us graciously, and invited us to lunch. But since we had to move on, we did not stay to eat. After a spot of tea, we set out for the Shkallë of Rrepës, which took us a long time to reach. On the way there we met a mother and daughter who were returning from the boarding school of Orosh, where they had gone to visit their son. They had been on the road for a day and a half! By and by we reached Orosh, which is a place of magnificent scenery. There are hills of varied contours covered with pine trees. *Mal i Shenjtë* (the Sacred Mountain), with its extremely steep, snow-capped peaks dominated the landscape, and enhanced its somewhat wild beauty.

We came to the knoll of the Church of Orosh, and one of our men pointed out the house of the *Kapedan*—located below the Mal' i Shenjtë—and the house of the *Bajraktar* of Orosh. The latter was built on top of a cone-shaped knoll, and had a very picturesque look. The Church of Orosh also was beautiful, and its large but now ruined parish house spoke well of the church's magnificent past.

We continued our trip downhill, and soon reached the church. Being a holy day, the people were celebrating mass. Our policeman, too, went inside to attend mass. We did not stop there long, however, since it was getting late. There was still another uphill climb ahead of us before we could get to the *Kapedan's* palace. Owing to the narrow and icy road—mostly because we were traveling through a dense forest—the horses had a very rough time. This gave our ill-tempered Zef a new opportunity to pour out a stream of profanity.

After much effort and trouble, we arrived at the courtyard of the *Kapedan's* house. He waited for us outside, and I lost no time in presenting him the foreign guests. Then he lead us to a room on the ground floor, where a huge fire was burning. The huge flames came from the pine wood that burned in the beautiful fireplace. The room was simple but clean. A blanket of goat's hair covered the floor. This time we sat on seats, rather than on the floor, as was the age-old custom. On the walls there hung a few rifles of warriors, and a large photograph.

After a while, two little children of the *Kapedan* came in and shook hands with us. One of the girls, named Bardhë, had a light complexion and golden hair. She was dressed in a white skirt, a velvet vest, and leather sandals. She was lively and quick as a little mountain goat.

An aide[26] served us coffee, and as he was serving us, and old woman came in, whom our host introduced as his mother. She took our hand, and in a gentle voice asked Prof. and Mrs. Coon: "How are you? Are you in good form? Are you tired?" She was well dressed, and her face mirrored a kind heart. Though raised in the highlands, she had the air of a lady of nobility. She left the room holding her hand over her heart, in the customary manner of the highlanders. Another woman, of large build, entered the room. It was the *Kapedan's* wife.

After spending some time in this room, the *Kapedan* proposed that we go to another room, in order to "relax." He led us to a room upstairs that was covered with a good carpet. The chamber had a lovely fireplace, a large table in the center, a wooden bed in one

---

26 The aides, called *trima*, which means "braves," were skilled riflemen or sharpshooters who served their tribal chief in a capacity of "bodyguards."

corner, a mirror, several photographs, and five or six European chairs. The windows were a little larger than usual for Mirditë homes, and they had panes. The fire in the room was roaring.

Mindful of our comfort, the *Kapedan* suggested that we take off our shoes and sit down on the floor, Albanian style. The Americans went along with the idea. Afterward Mrs. Coon put on a red blouse, which went well with her "beret."

"You are lucky," said our host. "You've had good weather. Otherwise, you would have been stranded for maybe a month in Orosh. The snow here reaches ten, fifteen feet, and then the horses cannot budge at all."

His words, however, did not ring true to me, for the weather was like summer. Even the snow that had fallen two weeks earlier, had melted because of the hot sun. Only on top of the mountains and in valleys where the sun did not shine was there a lot of snow.

It was time for dinner, and an aide of the *Kapedan* brought us a bottle of *raki* made from grapes, along with a plate of feta cheese. I had never seen such cheese before: it was so buttery. First one glass, then another, we emptied the bottle, and began to loosen up somewhat. The *Kapedan's* wife and mother kept moving about the room. And they kept asking Mrs. Coon whether she was "comfortable," and were quite attentive to her.

We finished our drinks, and the table was set for dinner. Our host invited us to be seated, and each one took his place.

"Tell these guests," he said to me, "to forgive us, because this is Mirditë, and we don't have the things they have in America." Upon hearing these words, Prof. Coon and his wife protested, gesturing with their hands and saying:

"*Jo, jo, shumë mirë! Shumë mirë*!" (No, no, very nice! Very nice!)

We were served soup, stewed chicken, broiled pork and pickles, buttery-white cheese, pilaf and a good wine. The women had just baked wheat bread on a clay pan, and served it to us oven-warm. The whole service was as good as it could be. We finished dining, thanked our host, washed our hands well, then drew close to the fireplace, which put one in a reflective mood. Again I recalled the warnings of my friends: wolves, bears, heavy snowfalls, lack of food, great discomfort! How far removed we were from such things!

They served us coffee again, we rolled up a cigarette, then began a pleasant chat. The *Kapedan* inquired about America: Does it have mountains and plains? How big is it? How do the people live there? etc. He had heard that in America it is night when we have daylight, and we assured him that it is so. For our part, we asked him many questions about Mirditë and its customs. He was the only person who could give us adequate and reliable information. Being the leader of a brave but unfortunate people, he understood the need for communications, schools, and the improvement of existing conditions, which were pitiful.

It was getting late, and Prof. Coon was yawning. The *Kapedan* then ordered that they prepare bedding for us. His aide provided me and Prof. Coon with two thick and soft mattresses and two nice big quilts. The sheets were from the Zadrimë region, and they were very clean. This time we did not have just a block of wood for a pillow, but a soft headrest in the true sense of the word. Our host, his mother, his wife and the aide all waited on us. Since we were all soiled from the journey, we hesitated to sleep on such good, clean linen. We decided that Mrs. Coon should sleep in bed and the two of us sleep near the corner by the fireplace. I and Prof. Coon began to undress in front of our hosts who had not yet quit the room. This became a great problem for Mrs. Coon, as she didn't dare undress in public! So she was obliged to go to bed with all her clothes on. When she got into bed, one of the women went over and covered her feet, like a good mother does with her children.

As soon as they left the room, Mrs. Coon got up giggling from her bed so as to undress. However she went quickly back to bed, when the aide came back to the room on some errand. When he went away, she got up again, did her customary toilette, undressed at her own leisure, then went to sleep.

We slept well all night, even though we had eaten a little too much. The room was well built to resist the elements, and as a result we did not feel the cold of Orosh at all. The next morning we got up somewhat late, in spite of the fact that we had work to do, as well as a long journey ahead of us. We got up, dressed up, washed our face, and drew close to the fire that the aide had lit up at dawn. The coffee was not long in coming.

After this formality, we took our measuring instruments and stepped out into the courtyard to measure the men of Orosh. We began with the aides of the *Kapedan* that were roaming about. Then we worked on a few other Orosh men, who were somewhat tardy in coming to be measured. They came to us upon being notified by our host. Like the others before them, these men also did not understand the purpose of measurements, and kept asking me constantly to explain.

Our quota had not yet been filled, and we were obliged to wait until a few more men came along for measurement. The sun had risen over the summit of the mountain and the beautiful hills of Orosh, enticing us to take some pictures. As happened before in Rras, here too one of the aides of the Kapedan became fond of Prof. Coon's rifle, and was eager to try it out. The American guest handed it to him with pleasure. The man then targeted a stone, pulled the trigger and smashed it to smithereens. These highlanders are terrible with a rifle! Hearing the shot, the *Kapedan's* mother came out of the house all upset, and asked: "What's that shot I heard?"

How could the poor woman help but be frightened? Who knows what terrible things her eyes had seen.

We would have stayed much longer in Orosh, but fearing that we might get caught in a big snowstorm, we decided to leave our host's house. The next destination was Fan.

Zef was bickering because he did not want to continue any longer on the trip. As a result, we found it necessary to hire new hands for our team at Orosh. In this connection, we became indebted to our host, who had the courtesy to provide us with three mules.

The new men got out our belongings together, and we made ready to start out anew. It was a relief to be rid of Zef. We said goodbye to the Kapedan, and thanked him for the warm welcome. Prof. Coon, in keeping with the local custom, gave our host's aide some change for the children. We thought it best to do this in an indirect way, so as not to embarrass that esteemed family. When we were about to depart, our host asked us to send him a telegram from Shkodër to assure him of our safe arrival there.

A red-faced, blond, blue-eyed and alert young man named Frok was entrusted by the *Kapedan* to head our caravan.

We departed from our host's home with much ceremony, and then began our trek along the foot of the Mal' i Shenjtë. The beauty of this place is indescribable. We passed through forests of pine trees measuring perhaps one meter in diameter and fifteen or more meters in height. The hand of nature had fashioned them in a most charming manner. They were truly living monuments of its work. As we trekked along, we had on our left the lofty Munellë mountain, which looked like a bride in a white veil. On our right there arose the steep and rocky face of Mal' i Shenjtë, all covered with pine wood and snow. One felt mad however to see that here and there tall willow trees had been cut down, merely to satisfy a whim. Had they used them, it would have been all right. Instead, they lay scattered about, most of them rotted. After a long march, we descended to the ford of the Little Fan river.

Leaving the ford, we crossed the terraced land of Bërzhanë, then pressed forward to its rugged gorge, in the middle of which flowed the Fan river, with its turbulent and foamy waters.

Not far from the gorge is Bisak, the first village one comes to in the district of Fan. We decided to look for lodgings here. After crossing a very dangerous bridge over the river, we arrived in town. Our policeman then led us to the house of the town's elder.

This good man welcomed us warmly, and we spent the night at his home. He had two children, a girl and a boy. The girl told us that she was a virgin[27] on account of her father and her only brother. She was about 22, and quite pretty. I assumed that she had remained a spinster because of an affair of the heart and not because she was sacrificing herself for the sake of her loved ones. I asked her about this, and she told me that in fact she had not married on account of her brother. She wanted to grow old together with him.

After measuring a few men in Fan, we bid goodbye to our host, with profuse thanks for his hospitality, and began to retrace our steps. Now Munellë mountain was on our right, while the Mal' i Shenjtë was on the left. Lunch time found us in the village of *Shëmëria* (St. Mary), where we made ourselves at home in an old church. A

[27] In those days, if a girl did not marry in her teens, she was considered a spinster, and to be a spinster meant in effect to be a virgin; hence the use of the term "virgin" by the girl.

highland lassie sold us a warm loaf of corn bread, which we ate in no time, along with some sardines and packaged butter from Europe. The brave lassie sold cheese as well, but she asked a lot for it, so we did not buy any. While walking uphill toward Spaç, we ran into "an honorable home," as our policeman used to put it. Here we met a woman who invited us over for a cup of coffee. It was here, too, that we bought a lovely and inexpensive pair of sox.

We left this hospitable home to resume our journey. As we followed the road, we kept climbing higher and higher. Whenever we thought we had reached the town of Spaç, another hill would rise up in front of us, and after that still another one! There was snow in certain spots along the way, and we took advantage of it by engaging in a snowball fight. The idea for the snowball fight came from Prof. Coon, who was proud of introducing this salutary custom to Mirditë, as a substitute for fights with bullets!!

Tired and worn out, we reached the hill of Spaç, in early twilight. From there we could see a cluster of houses in town. Our policeman pointed out a white building among the houses, and informed us that we were going to lodge there for the night. It was the house of Zef Noci, the renowned man of Mirditë.

When we arrived there, the policeman spoke to the lady of the house about our party. "Welcome, welcome," she said, and came out and shook hands with us. She moved in a leisurely fashion, and it was evident from her speech and bearing that she was used to receiving guests. "Zef Noci," the lads of Mirditë told me, "was a familiar name to the *shtatë kralat* (the seven kings);[28] it is a great and honorable family."

Following the ritual of the greetings, the woman led us to the men's parlor. The fire had been lit, and she gave Prof. and Mrs. Coon the place of honor by the fireplace. Although unfurnished, it was easy to see that the room must have been very attractive at one time, when the family had been prosperous. The mantelpiece of the chimney in this home was the most beautiful we had seen in Mirditë.

---

28 The "seven kings" refers to the seven major powers in Europe in the early part of the 20th century; namely, England, Germany, France, Italy, Austro-Hungary, Russia and Turkey.

We took off our shoes, and drew close to the hearth. Afterward a servant brought us coffee. Our hostess remained standing, with her hands crossed over her heart. Her two darling little children kept moving about the parlor and looking at us with amazement.

We did not bother our hostess about dinner, and instead prepared some soup ourselves. The household watched us make soup from a powdered mixture, and were astonished.

"Look at the way Europe does things!," commented the judicious woman. "We don't know how to live. We were born to suffer. Our children have no schooling at all."

As time passed, the two little boys became less shy and began to come closer to us. The older of the two smiled continually at us.

"They are orphans," their mother said, "and I'm afraid they won't be able to go to school. My oldest son," she continued, "is enrolled at the boarding school in Orosh."

After dining and drinking coffee, we went to sleep. Seeing, however, that I did not have any sleeping outfit, they provided me with comfortable bedding of their own for the night.

We got up very early in the morning, and began preparations to leave. Our hostess made coffee for us. We drank the coffee, thanked her and departed.

I learned later that this lady had an interesting past. And I believe that the reader would be interested to hear the story at this point.

It turns out that Zef Noci had been married once before, but had no offspring. He decided to take another wife—the lady who hosted us—even though he knew that the church would not allow it. So he eloped with the lady, and brought her home, and kept her there, along with his first wife, but took care not to let her step out of the house, for fear of being reviled by society.

This state of affairs lasted for some time. One day, however, he called the local priest to his home and told him everything. He pleaded with the priest to accept the marriage as a legitimate union, especially since he had a son by his second wife. The priest wrote the Pope for instructions, and the Pope not only rejected the marriage, but also ordered that Noci be excommunicated. The excommunication took place in the church, the "candles" were extinguished,[29] and consequently Zef was no longer permitted to take communion or to participate in the affairs of the church.

When he died, the church did not allow his family to bury him in the church-anointed burial ground, as was the custom. The people however got up at night and took his body from the grave where he had been buried, and interred him in church-anointed ground. The next day the priest had him exhumed and reburied in the first grave. The poor man! He was destined to suffer even in death.

A long time afterward, his widow was obliged to undergo a special type of punishment to escape excommunication. She had to carry a huge stone on her back, and go around the church building three times, and then stand before the congregation, while the priest struck her three times on the back with a "rod." In this manner the church received once again a brave woman, who had known much pain and suffering in her life.

We passed the time on the road talking about this and other things, when shortly we came to Plagëz, a village of only five houses. We decided to eat lunch here, and measure a few men as well.

At this point, the son of the innkeeper at Ungrej called out to a man who was standing by his house and watching us: "Hey, man, come on over to be measured, and bring over a few sheaves of hay for the mules!"

And truly the old fellow came, bringing with him the hay for the animals. To my surprise, I learned later that our men had not paid anything for the hay, because the custom in Mirditë would not allow it. Imagine! To be measured and to bring feed, too, and yet not get even a *dyshkë* (old Turkish coin) in return! That's going the extra mile, as the saying goes. All that the old man received during the time we stayed in his village was two packages of European butter and a bottle of beer. But he was very happy with it all, and told me that he was using the beer bottle to put whiskey in it.

We finished our work at Plagëz, and set out slowly for Kalivar.

---

29 The ritual of excommunication involved the extinction of candles in the church, to symbolize apparently the extinction from the body and life of the church of the excommunicated person.

"We will spend the night over at the priest's house," our mule drivers said to me. "He treats his guests well."

The Munellë mountain still followed us, as it were, along the way. And it was interesting to observe it from different vantage points, for at each point it seemed to take a different form. As we traveled, we had on our left the Rranzi Mountain, the Great Crest of Spaç, and the *Qafë e Shenjtë* (Sacred Pass). Presently we came to the Spaç mountain, and from there descended to the village of Mesul.

A short time before arriving in Kalivar, Prof. Coon told me that he had lost his wallet, and that he had some money in it. This upset us all, even after he informed us that the wallet contained not more than one hundred gold francs. He was certain that he had the wallet with him when we left Zef Noci's house. He feared that he might have dropped it while bending down for a drink of water at some spring along the road. We therefore sent Frok to go back and see if he might find it somewhere.

We continued on our path, making our way between the Domi mountains on the left and the Këmëzë mountains on the right. We came thus to the Monastery of Kalivar, which is about fifteen minutes away from the village of Kalivar.

Our pack animals stopped in the courtyard of the house of the parish priest, and the policeman in our team called out to the servant on duty. A moment later this saintly-looking elderly man came out. He did not smile, held his hands over his heart, and was reluctant to talk. The policeman explained to him the purpose of our visit, but from what I heard he did not want to accommodate us.

"I have no place for the animals," he was saying. "And what feed I have isn't enough even for the livestock of the parish house."

Just then another servant showed up, a smiling boy of perhaps fourteen. He was not a pharisee-type like the old man. Seeing that we were in a tight spot, he said briskly: "Sir, I'll find a place for two of your mules. The others you can leave in the village."

It may be that the old man did not like the idea of the kind-hearted lad, but he was forced to go along with his suggestion.

Two of the men in our party did not want to go to Kalivar because they were afraid they would not find shelter there. I heard later that the inhabitants of Kalivar and those of Orosh—the home of our mule driver's—were not too hospitable to each other.

We unloaded the animals, and the men carried our belongings to the bedroom. The room had three beds, a table, a stand with a wash basin for washing the face, and a few photographs of the priest and his family.

Prof. Coon and his wife stayed in the bedroom until dinner time, while I went down to the kitchen, where I found four or five men, all seated by the fireplace. The parish father had stocked up well for the winter, as was clear form the chunks of ham, salted meat and cabbages that hung from the ceiling. A casserole dish was cooking over the fire. The kitchen was lighted by a small kerosene lamp and the light of the fireplace.

The servant set the table and called us to dinner. As in the house of the *Kapedan*, so here too the service was quite good. They brought us *raki*, feta cheese, broiled pork, fried eggs, wheat bread, pickles, plus good wine. We stuffed ourselves. To better digest the food, the old man served us coffee, as well.

After dinner, the Americans went upstairs to sleep, while I headed for the kitchen to chat with the men who were seated by the fire.

A long-nosed mason with the face of a Gypsy, who worked in the parish grounds, entertained us with fables and jokes of all sorts. Another dictated some old Mirditë songs to me.

The young who helped to shelter us had a deck of cards, and wanted to play a game. And so we did, in spite of the fact that he could not tell one card from another.

I went to bed very late that night, because I enjoyed the company of those simple men.

The roosters of the monastery awoke us at dawn, and the "holy man" brought us water to wash our face. For breakfast he served us only coffee, even though I had sent word to him indirectly that the American couple liked to have a fried egg or two, along with some bits of broiled pork. We also wanted to buy some meat at the parish house, since we could not find any among the poor highlanders in the vicinity. But here again our request fell on deaf ears. This establishment was known to be one of the wealthy institutions in Mirditë. It had a good building and plenty of livestock, corn, and other provisions. All that was needed was people with a true Christian spirit.

Unfortunately, the parish priest was absent, otherwise, we might have had a better reception than the one given us by the Pharisee servant.

We completed here our quota for measurements of the men in Mirditë. It was time to go to Pukë. As word of our plan spread around, we began to hear warnings, such as: "Pukë is the worst region of Albania; people freeze to death there." I had heard in Tiranë that when the Government wanted to punish a soldier, they made him walk all the way to Pukë! But who paid attention to such warnings? We were determined to go there, come hell or high water. So we simply ignored such old wives' tales.

Moments before departing, a Mirditë man with a rifle on his shoulder came up to me and said: "Who are these strangers? Do they know German? How is that woman related to this man?" etc.

In order not to hurt his feelings, I answered all his questions, and as a result we became friends.

"I learned German when the Austrians were here," he said. "I've been in Vienna, too."

He was the third or the fourth man we had met in Mirditë up to that time who knew how to read and write Albanian! He had some progressive ideas, as well. He said: "The roads are bad. But what can be done to repair them? We don't pay any taxes to the Government. So, where is the money going to come from to fix the roads? I am the elder in my village; but the villagers don't pay attention to me. They think I'm a fool!"

After giving a tip to the old servant and the young fellow at the parish house, we left the holy place. The modern but superficial Mirditë man came along with us. Now and then he conversed with Prof. Coon in German, but I could not understand what they were saying.

We were well along the way when he turned to me and said:

"Will you tell the American to exchange revolvers with me?"

"Oh, no," I said, "I couldn't tell him that. He is very fond of that six-shooter."

Then he proposed something else to me. "Can't you tell him to send me a *tyrbi*[30] from America? I'll give him something in return."

---

30 *Tyrbi*, a dialect form for the word dylbi—binoculars, field glasses. Possession of a pair of binoculars would have made him a distinguished man.

I squelched this hope of his as well, telling him that these foreign guest were not millionaires, as he supposed. Happily, he left our party when we reached the ford of the Big Fan. We parted exchanging a thousand and one expressions of courtesy, but in fact I had become bored with him, and had feared that he might come up with other proposals such as those mentioned above.

Luck was with us in crossing the Fan. The water was low; otherwise we could not have made it across the stream, which in places was rather deep. We feared the current might carry off one of the mules, including the instruments the beasts carried on their backs, without which we could do nothing.

With our hearts beating fast—for one gets dizzy crossing an impetuous stream on the back of a mule—we managed to reach the other side in safety. The mule drivers forded the stream stripped naked down to the waist.

With the Fan river behind us, we began an uphill climb which took us to Gojan. On the way there we came across a terribly battered old man. I will speak of him later, in another chapter. As we traveled, we could see the mountain of Gojan and the peak of Suçel to our left. We climbed higher and higher, drawing closer with each step to the Pukë-Mirditë border line.

The mule drivers were getting restless now. They told me that we were entering an unfriendly region, and therefore the pay they were receiving was not enough, considering the risks they would be taking. It is true that during our trip through Mirditë we met a few people who had lost the virtue of hospitality. It is true also that the evil spirit of commercialism had penetrated a few places in the region. In general, however, the Mirditë native welcomes and honors the guest who enters his home, and offers him whatever the Lord has provided, without giving any thought to recompense on the part of the guest. As for the mule drivers, they had a right to feel uneasy, since they were convinced that henceforth they would not find highlanders to whom they could say aloud: "Come on out to be measured, and bring along a few sheaves of hay, too."[31]

---

31 The author does not tell us how the issue was resolved, but since he appears to sympathize with the drivers, they were probably given a raise in wages.

A cold wind was blowing at this altitude. The policeman accompanying us told me that we had reached the Rrapës pass, beyond which lay Pukë. The first village we came to in this area was Ryp. It was obvious from the *xhami* (mosque) and the burial ground that we had left the borders of Mirditë. The mule drivers were hungry, and one of them, overcoming his misgivings, walked up to a house nearby in search of something to eat. He came back empty-handed, in spite of the fact that he had offered to pay for the food.

Commenting on the weather, our policeman said to me: "You're lucky. The weather is on your side. For it is very difficult to cross the Rrapës pass in winter. The snow reaches fifteen to twenty feet here in winter!"

"What!" I said. "Fifteen feet, you say! Is that really true?"

I could hardly believe him, though I noticed that in some places the old snow had not melted as yet, and in fact it was still many inches deep.

Walking and chatting along the way, we came to the Inn of Rrapës, where we planned to stay for the night. Here we were going to start measuring men from a new district—the notorious district of Pukë. And so we bid goodbye to Mirditë, taking with us very beautiful memories and impressions.

11
Health

To be ill in Mirditë is to be in real trouble, especially if the illness is serious. Doctors, pharmacists and other medical help is lacking. I assure you that if a man is taken ill suddenly, and needs immediate medical care, he is a lost soul. How can a sick man make a two-day journey to Lezhë to see a doctor? Besides the roads are so bad, he would expire sooner if he undertook the journey, than if he stayed at home. We, urban dwellers, are fortunate to have the doctor at our doorstep in case of need. As a result, we probably don't realize what it means to have a loved one laid out ill, and not be able to help him, but only watch him vanish in front of your eyes. And what if there is an epidemic? You can imagine what happens then!

I had heard many people say that the greater part of the highlands was inundated by venereal diseases. However, I wanted to check to see if this report was true, so I observed carefully the men who came to us to be measured. I can say that not even two percent of those we examined in Mirditë showed any symptoms of syphilis.

As for dental hygiene, the highlanders generally had bad teeth.

I was impressed by the many scars I saw on the hands of these people—scars caused by gunshot wounds. I was impressed also by the fact that many of them were short a finger.

I noticed that many suffered from smallpox, were pale from malaria or had an enlarged spleen. Wherever we went they asked us for medicine for the heart, for malaria, for headaches, etc. Our medical services would have known no bounds, had we had the medicine to give to those in need of it. Thinking we were doctors, they kept telling us about the illness of this or that poor highlander, and asking for medicine for the patient.

The hard life they live because of poverty, the lack of doctors and medicaments, and ignorance about the most elementary principles of hygiene, cost the lives of a great number of people who might otherwise be useful citizens.

There is great need for the establishment of two or three infirmary stations, where this wretched people could be treated properly, instead of being left in the hands of witches who dispatch their patients to the other world all the sooner.

This kind of care is at present given by a kind-hearted priest here and there; but it is not enough. What is needed are medical specialists with the requisite professional equipment.

I learned that infant mortality was high. This is not surprising when you consider that the infants' mothers are ignorant and under the influence of the old women, have little time to look after their children, know nothing about infant health care, let the children run around naked because they are too poor to clothe them, and do not feed them properly.

12

Education

During our entire stay in Mirditë, we encountered no more than five persons who could read and write. One of them was a soldier, the second a little boy who had been taught by a friar, the third a villager in Kalivar, and the other two had picked it up here and there. To be literate in Mirditë is no small accomplishment. The natives believed that writing was magic! Seeing Mrs. Coon write down the words spoken by her husband in the course of his research, they would say, "Look, look how the wife is able to write down what her husband says!"

It is useless to speak of education in Mirditë, since it does not exist. The only source of enlightenment in the region is the *Internati* (boarding school) of Orosh, with an enrollment of about 100 students. Unfortunately, this institute has benefited only those who have had connections. As a result, many capable youth and children of poor families may have been excluded.

At any rate, a single school in a region of approximately 18,000 people, scattered far and wide, cannot bear much fruit. In general boarding schools are designed for poor children and for those who can afford to pay, and their enrollments are limited. This is especially true of Mirditë, where the expenses are great, on account of the high cost of materials.

The educational problem that confronts Mirditë shows up of course in other highland areas as well. What is to be done?

We see that boarding schools are not practical, since they are very expensive, and consequently not enough of them can be built to meet the needs of the population.

Most of the villagers in Mirditë have churches whose priests are highly educated. Those honorable men could be entrusted with the task of educating the population, particularly since it is their duty to do so. On the other hand, it may be feared that those gentlemen might drown the children in religious fanaticism, instead of giving them scientific knowledge. Such a development could be ruinous for our country. The Government, therefore, should exercise close control over education in situations of this sort.

We have already mentioned that houses in the villages of Mirditë stand far apart from one another, and there are cases where the church might be two hours away on foot from the home of a pupil. Two hours to go to class, and two hours to return. How much time is left to him for learning?

Therefore, until the time comes when the villages in Mirditë become more compact, another solution is called for. A long time ago, Norway's highlands were in the same condition as ours are today. Norway's solution to the problem of education in its highlands was as follows: Since it was not possible for the children to attend school, because it was too far from their homes, the state adopted the system of the "ITINERANT TEACHER." This teacher would go from village to village and instruct the children for brief periods of time. This way everyone had the chance to learn reading and writing, and, what is more, how to improve their own lot. Can't we also organize groups of itinerant teachers to educate our youth, who are impatiently looking for light?

Following are some of the remarks I heard in this poor land:

"I'm afraid that my children will be left without schooling." So said a mother to me in Spaç.

"Take me to school in Tiranë," a young man implored me.

"Please send my only child to school," pleaded an old man.

"*Nuk kena shkolla*" (We don't have no schools)—this was the constant refrain of people.

It is fortunate that the highlanders have begun to sense that the time of the rifle is gone, and that their salvation will come from education. This is a good sign which should give heart to every progressive-minded person, even though very little has been done in Mirditë toward that end.

To conclude this discussion, I say that friars endowed with a patriotic conscience plus itinerant teachers would be able to tear off the veil of darkness that covers this land that is so thirsty for knowledge. The construction of three, four or five boarding schools would not solve the problem of education in Mirditë.

13

How the Mirditë People Occupy Themselves

The men of Mirditë have been skillful at "pulling the trigger." Consequently, both in ancient and more recent times they have been a source of manpower for fighting armies. Their clan leaders used those armies for various purposes. They also promised a small monthly or periodic compensation to the fighting men for their services.

One day in Ungrej, among the men who came to be measured, there were also two old men, one of whom was short an ear, while the other had a glass eye. I asked them what had happened, and both told me that they had been wounded in Durrës while fighting for the Prince Wied. One of them talked boastfully about those past events, and said that some three hundred men from Mirditë had taken part in the operations. He said that in return they were given 3 *napolon* (gold coins) per man. From his account it is clear that the men who bore arms were used as mercenaries. Apart from the compensation they received, they could also engage in plunder, whose extent depended on the victim's bounty.

As soon as a strong Government came to power and collected all guns held by civilians, the highlanders began to think and started to go into farming. That is why today, if you ask someone what he does, he no longer answers, "I pull the trigger," but rather, "I'm a farmer."

The terrain of Mirditë is generally mountainous, but the rain, the sun and other forces are doing their job at eroding and transforming the fierce character of this rugged land. Even so, a long time will pass before this land takes on the shape of rolling hills.

The farmer in Mirditë is in bad shape, because he has to work with narrow parcels of craggy and rocky soil. Since the tilled land runs along the foot of the mountains, the rains wash off the top soil and dump it onto the rivers. As a result, the tilled land becomes impoverished and insufficiently productive. Often chunks of rock roll off from the mountain side unto the farm land, making the job of tilling difficult. The rocks are removed, but new ones take their place, and so the job of clearing the land continues "ad infinitum."

What little flat land there is, is to be found along the rivers and brooks. Such land is the result of soil deposits swept down from the mountains by the rains, and carried forward by the rivers and brooks.

Apart from a few large homesteads and monasteries, the average farm in the highlands may have enough arable to employ 3 to 5 teams of oxen,[32] and yield 10 to 12 loads[33] of corn, totaling 1,000–1,200 kilograms. A farmland of this size is not sufficient to meet the annual food needs of a large family.

The farm and the meadows in the highlands are adjacent to one's home. The soil is tilled by means of a plow drawn by oxen.

If a family lacks oxen, it can hire them by paying 3 to 4 loads of corn (300–400 kg.) for four teams of oxen. Unfertilized soil is not very productive, and this can be said of most of the farms in the region. Since they have only a few heads of livestock, they don't have much fertilizer either to use on their farms. In such cases, a farmer may get a yield of not more than 5 to 6 kg. of corn for every kg. that he plants.

Owing to the absence of good, rich soil only certain kinds of cereals are planted in Mirditë. All of the highlanders without exception plant corn. It was only at the home of the priest, and at another home that we found wheat bread. However, since the families in this region are quite large, no corn is left over to sell in the market. Indeed, many times there is not even enough to meet the needs of one's own family. The planting is done in April; the harvesting in Autumn.

Wherever we went, we heard complaints about the lack of water in the month of August.

"We don't have irrigation," they said. "The corn grows, then dries up and falls to the ground." Happy is he who grows all the food he needs.

Some areas are very suitable for planting potatoes. But when we spoke about this subject, they answered: "We've never done it before; we're not used to eating potatoes; it's not our habit to plant potatoes."

---

[32] Plowing in prewar Albania was generally done by teams of oxen, each team consisting of two animals.

[33] A load or *barrë* was the amount carried by a pack animal, the weight varying according to circumstances.

As we have already seen on another occasion, it is characteristic of the Mirditë highlander to have a garden for planting tobacco, cabbages, onions, leeks, cucumbers, tomatoes and other vegetables. The planting of such items depends mostly on the availability of water.

It would be a good thing if they planted a variety of fruit trees, inasmuch as their yield could be a very good source of food. In this manner, not only would the top soil of the tilled land not erode when it rains, but the soil itself would benefit from the fallen leaves. Where corn is planted at present, it would be more profitable to plant apple trees, walnut trees, chestnut trees, almond trees, etc. Let us not forget that the food value of such trees is not insignificant. Carob trees could be planted as well, and be utilized as food for pigs. If the highlanders worked in this fashion, they would improve their own lot and that of the nation as well.

Since farming in Mirditë cannot progress under existing conditions, the highlanders have turned their attention to livestock instead. Livestock breeding makes up for the defects of an inhospitable land. For example, if a family should fail to grow enough food crops to last through the year, then in order to get through the winter, it could sell a few heads of livestock, or borrow what it needs from another house at one hundred percent interest. Moreover, sheep, lambs and goats can graze on land that is not arable. This is especially true of goats which can climb to places where the foot of man can never tread. In the summer these animals seek the heights of the mountains, while in the winter they come down to feed on reserves that the highlanders stock up in advance.

In general the pastures belong to the village as a whole, and everyone sends his livestock to graze on those plots. They are very careful not to overstep the bounds of the designated plots, for fear of getting into trouble with a neighboring village. The grass of the meadows is cut down in June, and happy is the family that is able to secure sufficient feed for its livestock. The hay is sold at 20 *para* per *okë*.[34] Here and there in the mountains of Mirditë are to be seen "haystacks" of oak leaves, which serve as feed for the livestock in the winter. Often these stacks are situated so high up in the mountains that one

---

34 The *para* was the lowest unit of currency at the time; the *okë* was a measuring unit equaling 1,408 kg.

wonders how it is possible for anyone to get to them, especially when the snow is knee-deep high. More power to the sturdy legs of the Mirditë women! Besides hay and oak leaves, during winter the livestock are fed fern, pine leaves, cornstalks and juniper, depending on what is most on hand.

Rare are the homes that sell their dairy products. They don't have much livestock to begin with, so that if a new head is added to the herd, they have the choice of selling it, if necessary—rather than its produce—in exchange for bread.

There are mountains in Mirditë that are completely bare—just rock formations in the process of decomposition. Perhaps at one time they had some kind of trees. There are other mountains that are covered with a variety of trees, mostly pine and beech in the higher altitudes, and oak, hornbeam, juniper, etc. in the lower altitudes.

The forest is the property of the village, and every family has the right to cut as much wood as it needs—within a designated area—for fuel, building materials, etc. One day I noticed a pile of wood on a hill, with a few stones on top. I asked a Mirditë native to tell me about the wood and the stones. He said the stones signified that the wood belonged to the person who had cut it; hence, no one could put his hands on that pile of wood.

If there were roads in Mirditë, the forests would have great value. Unfortunately, the cost of transporting the wood from the forest is prohibitive, and as a consequence the forests remain unexploited.

The forests are getting smaller day by day because of lack of control. Anyone can cut wood according to his fancy, without taking into account the harm he may be doing. The trouble is that they think only of today and not of tomorrow. Water-powered sawmills are nonexistent. Lumber is cut with a hatchet. Big trees are felled to the ground for lumber. It is pitiful to see that over half of the wood that is cut down is wasted, simply by being left behind to rot on the ground. Even when they cut wood for fuel, they cut the trees in such a manner as to stunt their growth for a long time to come.

Let us look now at some other destructive factors, in connection with forests. When there is a fierce storm, the saplings are completely crushed by big trees felled by the storm. No one in the village cares about the preservation of the communal forest, on which they depend for many things.

Shepherds are also destructive, since they set fire unwittingly to forests, and threaten them with total extinction. Lightning is another cause of forest fires. With the extinction of the forest comes the impoverishment of the land, owing, as we said earlier, to the erosion of the top soil by rain.

Nor should we forget that even goats are capable of undoing a fledging forest. This simple creature loves green twigs and leaves, and climbs branch upon branch to get at them. As a result, no chance is given to the young forest to grow to maturity, and the village that owns the forest suffers the consequences without being aware of it.

Of the forests I saw in Mirditë, those of Orosh stand out for their beauty. I saw pine trees there 15-20 meters tall, and as much as 80 cm. wide. Unfortunately, the ax of the villager has no mercy. Tall oaks, supposedly cut down for lumber, are seen lying on the ground and ravaged by the elements. Here and there one sees pine trees whose trunk has been chipped off at the base by a villager for the sake of a few splinters of wood. There are no regulations in force. Consequently, these monuments of nature—which could attract many people, once road communications are available—are disappearing day by day. Is it not possible for the communes and the police force to protect these forests, which promise to be an inestimable treasure in the time to come? How beautiful are the lofty mountains when they are clothed with forests! It is a pity to have them and not know their worth. If some European country had such forests, you would see what use they would make of them.

Commerce in the region is at low level. Being poor, the people are not able to buy much merchandise, and in place of currency they resort to barter, exchanging such articles as stockings, sweaters, sneaker sox, gloves, etc., as well as corn, eggs, chickens, animal skins and other things. There is no market for finished goods as such. Lezhë and Shkodër have markets for goods of that sort, but the villagers rarely travel to those commercial centers. The first reason is that they don't have surplus goods for sale, and secondly the two towns are too far. The inns with stores, however, that are scattered about the area, manage to do some business handling goods of this kind.

In such inns, the villagers buy rice, coffee, sugar, a cake of soap, dried sardines, yarn for knitting socks, dye, thread, ribbons, oil, corn, bullets (in former times), and other basic necessities. It often happens that the shopkeeper cheats them, by taking advantage of their ignorance of buying and selling. If they don't have cash, this honorable gent sells them merchandise on credit, receiving payment at harvest time at 100 to 120 percent interest! The rate depends on the "magnanimity" of the dealer!

Industry also is very backward, because of problems of transportation, the isolation of the region, and the fact that the men are not "accustomed" to work much. The women however are quite industrious, and use wool to make stockings, sneaker sox, sweaters, gloves, white trousers trimmed with black, as well as clothing for themselves and for the children, and other items needed for the house.

A family that has land but no hands to work it is obliged to hire laborers from the village and pay them by the day or by the year. Such a laborer may receive 2 *okë* (aprox. 3 kg.) of corn per day, or 200–300 *korona* (crowns) plus meals, if he works by the year. He may also be paid in bread grains.

The "division of labor" in Mirditë is very undeveloped. The highlanders work at all sorts of jobs, with the result that none of them is able to achieve mastery at a particular craft.

Those who have a trade are better off than those who till the land. The blacksmith, the carpenter, the stonemason, etc., keep more or less busy.

"A carpenter who once worked on the bridges of Mirditë," they would say, "is now a gentleman; he is in demand everywhere."

But in a land with a poor and spread-out population, even the craftsmen cannot get very far. They work off and on. If they own a bit of land, they can work on the farm when they are not working at their trade. But this means that they cannot concentrate on their trade, and the natural result is that they fall behind.

The highlander works a little on the farm, in the summer, while in winter he is an idle consumer of the provisions he had laid up in summer. He thus fails to develop certain positive qualities in his makeup that regular work would foster or make possible. In Rras we found a carpenter-artist who did good work. He asked for 2 *napolon* (gold coins) for a carved seat, and Prof. Coon ordered two of them. This proves that he had artistic taste which could have been developed to an even higher degree, if he had a market for his products.

We have seen that the worker is paid for in bread grains, and this is true also of the blacksmith who hones farming tools. This man receives 9–18 kg. of corn a year for his labors. The miller receives 4–6 percent of the total volume of grains milled, while the priest is given 25 kg. of corn a year for his services.

In olden times, when there was no law and order in the land, the men of Mirditë from time to time came down from the mountains, gun in hand, and raided the peaceful Zadrimë. This region was the victim of the hungry and idle men of Mirditë. Fortunately this does not happen anymore, except for a sheep or a goat that is stolen during the summer season.

The job of policeman apparently appeals to the folk of Mirditë, since a great number of them have made it their profession. The irony of it is that the present guardian of the law may have been an outlaw before. In spite of that, he does his job as well as possible. Doesn't this show that even law breakers can be transformed into useful agents of society?

The Mirditë man has had no desire to immigrate. He left his home only in case of war. Today you see him working in Mat as a lumberman, farmer, craftsman, servant, etc. You see him at work on roads, exploit mineral resources, etc. Is this not a radical change for him?

This land abounds in wildlife, and affords good opportunities to the zealous hunter. The wolf is found in many places, and during Winter becomes quite dangerous as it attacks livestock. Here and there one finds deer and wild goats. Bears are rare. There are also foxes, wild boars, and other small but unimportant game.

The main rivers in Mirditë are the Big Fan and the Little Fan, both of which run strong when it rains in the summer or winter; otherwise, they don't have much water in the summer season. There are in addition a great number of other streams, but these dry up in the summer. They come to life in winter, and then they flow impetuously and are dangerous. If the mountains were covered with forests, these streams would not become so swollen with water, since a portion of the water from the rains would be absorbed by soil underneath the trees.

We saw a large number of waterfalls, too, but I think that most of them disappear when the winter is over.

Water power resources have not been developed at all, even though the possibilities for its development are great. One sees primitive flour mills everywhere. Only in Fan did we see a more or less sophisticated fulling mill. Although primitive in construction, this mill was sound in principle. If it were located in an industrial country, it could well inspire the construction of a more advanced machine complex of this nature.

The farming tools used by the Mirditë people are primitive. The wooden parts of such tools are made by the farmers themselves, while the metal parts are made for them by the local blacksmith. Some of these tools are: the hoe, the pick, the pitchfork, the plow, the hook, a large wicker basket (for transporting manure), the harrow (for crumbling chunks of soil), stakes, stretchers, the adz, the hatchet, the billhook (for cutting thorn bushes), the scythe, an implement for cutting corn, etc.

The consumption of food in the region is inadequate; yet the people are relatively healthy. The lack of mental exertion, plus the fact that most of the time they work and live in a clear outdoor environment, makes them seem strong and healthy. The Mirditë natives eat mostly corn, meat, milk, cheese, pork, beans, salad greens, various vegetables, and baked dishes like *pite me kungull* (pumpkin pie), and *pite me hinjth* (a vegetable pie).[35] These are nourishing foods, except that they are not consumed in sufficient quantities. Meat is eaten only rarely, since by so doing the highlanders have a chance to increase their heads of livestock, or to replace those that die or are eaten by wolves. Another reason for sparing the animals is to sell them in the market place, in case of need, in order to buy essential goods.

Do not imagine that the life of the shepherd is easy, even though he leads a life of leisure when the weather is good. The night we spent in Blinisht at the home of an old woman, her nephew came over and told her that a wolf had attacked the sheep. Happily the beast had not done any damage. Wolves, heavy snows, the crossing of a torrential river, etc. are things that would inflict the *ethet e Gushtit* (malarial

[35] Hinjth is a local form for *hithër* — nettle (Lat. *Urtica).* This is a green plant about 60-90 cm. high, whose leaves are sufficiently toxic to cause blisters on the skin. Yet when dried or baked, this plant, so rude to the touch when it's fresh, makes a delicious pie.

fever in August)[36] upon a city dweller who has never stepped beyond the threshold of his home. To say nothing of the situation the highlander finds himself in when he is in a blood feud with a fellow villager. Life for the highlander is full of troubled excitement. But this sort of thing has toughened his hide, and he laughs at a city dweller who becomes cautious over trivial matters.

The wretchedness of the Mirditë people reveals itself in different ways: in their ragged clothing and naked feet, the lack of adequate food and drink, the lack of cleanliness, and in their stark bare houses. In other words, their life is a struggle to keep body and soul together. A long and hard winter would suffice to wipe out a considerable number of this unfortunate people.

Whenever Mirditë and other highland regions have had a bad year, the Government and charity organizations have helped them with food. This job has been done as well as possible, but the highlanders may some time seek aid on a mere pretext. If that happens, we shall have a group of parasites in our midst, which will be generally harmful to the country.

There is no doubt that arable land in this region is both limited in area and poor in quality. Even so, I believe that there may be some bread grains especially suitable for planting in this soil, whose yield would satisfy the annual food needs of the villagers. The land must be cultivated more intensively, in order to make it truly productive. Only then will the villagers be rid of the fear of not knowing where their next meal is going to come from.

The new agronomists who are full of idealism have a wide open field of study awaiting them. They can solve the agricultural problem in Mirditë, on which the happiness of its people depends. Let us not forget, too, that the Presidents of the Communes could do a lot for this poor land.

The wretched condition that prevails at present shall disappear only when suitable crops are planted in the impoverished soil, and when roads are built and schools are opened; when men spend less time discussing "politics," and more time working with all their

---

[36] Malaria was the most common and most ravaging disease in prewar Albania. It afflicted its victims usually in the summer months. The phrase *ethet e Gushtit*, therefore connoted a dreadful experience.

might, and lastly, when the leaders of Mirditë stop trying to profit from the ignorance of the people and using them for their own ends, as happened in former times. Much human energy goes to waste when used in that manner. But with good leadership, all that energy could be applied toward their common salvation. Schools, roads, and idealistic workers—that's what "forlorn Mirditë" needs today.

14

The Clergy and the Clan Leaders

It will seem paradoxical to the reader to be told that the people of Mirditë accept blindly what their clergy tell them, yet do no put their preaching into practice. The Catholic clergy is educated and influential among the masses. Nevertheless, one is astounded at the lack of progress in the region. Darkness is at the zenith, the standards of cleanliness are lower than those of their Moslem neighbors, religious fanaticism is at its maximum, while the practice of the tenets of the faith is, I'm afraid, at the minimum. In brief, life in Mirditë is miserable.

From what I heard and saw, the priest in Mirditë is respected very much. He is respected either because of his role as a wise counselor in all matters of concern to the faithful—which is fine—or because they think that the priest communes with the Lord, and is the only being who can assure them a place in Heaven! The Mirditë man is wily, and does not want to be on bad terms with the agent who has been entrusted with the "ministry of the Faith." Fear guards the vineyard, as the saying goes, and therefore the highlander fears the Reverend Father, although there are times when he ignores him completely.

Journeying from Kalivar to the Rrapës Pass, we met an old mountaineer on the road—we referred to him earlier—who was in the worst possible shape. The flesh of his body could be seen through his ragged clothes. He was weak from hunger, and black from being unwashed. He had one foot in the grave and the other outside.

After Prof. Coon and his wife moved some distance away, I drew near this simple man and asked him: "What are you doing here?"

"*Tunjatjeta! Tunjatjeta!* (Long life to you, long life to you), I'm not doing anything," replied the miserable old man, placing his hands on his forehead, as a gesture of courtesy.

When I told him, "Don't be afraid, I won't hurt you," the wretch said to me:

"I just paid my annual debt to the priest. I gave him the 25 kg. of corn I owed him."

About fifty meters ahead of us, the servant of the priest was returning to Kalivar with a mule loaded with corn. The old man pointed him out to me, all the while shivering from the cold.

"Is it possible," I asked myself, "that the priest would take corn from this man! Has he ever seen him?" Then I thought of the parish house in Kalivar, and how well supplied it was with all good things: meat, vegetables, corn, cheese, good wine, etc. What a contrast with the house of this old man! How can the soul of man help but revolt against such a thing? What would Christ have done if he were alive?

I turned to the old man and said: "My good man, how can you give corn to the priest when you yourself are going around in rags? You're on the way to the grave, old fellow."

"By God," he answered, "one must pay his debt to the priest; otherwise he won't bury you and perform last rites for you. One must give the priest his due, even if he has to go into debt. We are a poor people, it's true, but we believe that debts should be paid."

I gave him a few cigarettes, then walked away from the miserable creature. I pondered his words, just as anyone else in my place would have done. But to come to the point. This story shows clearly that the Mirditë highlander fears the priest. Otherwise, why should it matter to an ignorant man if his corpse is buried in unhallowed ground and without benefit of last rites!

The clan leaders behave in the same way as the clergy. But whereas the priests are men of learning, these men are not. They have always taken advantage of opportunities that came their way, and capitalized on the respect their family line enjoyed. The Mirditë man attaches great importance to genealogy, and believes obstinately that he should follow his clan leader. One hears constantly the phrase:

"*Asht prej shpije të madhe*" (He comes from a noble family). Nor does he question the competence of the clan leader. In the old days there were no elections by vote for clan leaders, as there are at present under the current legal system. The right of inheritance was enough to settle the matter, as far as the highlanders of former times were concerned.

This attachment to the past shows itself in our day during communal elections. Election results prove that Mirditë highlanders favor as counselors men of rank whose positions of leadership have been handed down from father to son for generations. It will take time to get rid of this primitive mentality. For if you try to push the highlander to make reforms, he will think you are acting against his interests and can be dangerous.

Inasmuch as not the slightest progress has been made in Mirditë in the course of many centuries, we can say that clan leaders until now have cared more for their own interests than for the welfare of the people they led. They claimed in self-defense that they merely strived to protect their lawful privileges, but in reality they worked to secure ever greater wealth for their houses. Under their leadership many men lost their lives or were maimed, ostensibly for the sake of a better future. But what has been the outcome, in reality? The people paid an inestimable price with their own blood, while their leaders increased their material gains.

Happily for the Mirditë people themselves, as well as for the whole of Albania, today one hears on occasion remarks such as:

"We've been fools. We've slain and battered one another in vain. Our houses have been burned, leaving us shelter-less. What did we gain from all this? Nothing! The houses of our leaders were burned, too, but they replaced them with mansions! We've been blockheads."

Mirditë is a place where the idealistic priest and the conscientious clan leader can perform miracles.

15

Mirditë Humor

Although the Mirditë highlanders live a hard life, they do not go about with a long face, as if the dog had raided their pantry. It's not as if they wait impatiently for someone to make them smile. This subject brings to mind the jokes I heard when they came to be measured by Prof. Coon. Here are some of them.

One day I asked a man, "How many times has your father married?"

"Never!" he replied.

In answer to the same question, another man said, "My father has been married once, and even then against his will!"

All who heard him died laughing.

When a midget came over to be measured, a mustached highlander burst out with the remark: "Oh, friend, don't you measure that guy or you'll pollute the entire country. This guy is a gypsy!"

I asked him how many sons did the midget's father have, and he replied: "His father had one son and a half. And this one is not the half!"

While making measurements of the highlanders, Prof. Coon reported the findings to his associate in a uniform tone of voice, not unlike that of a priest performing mass. This prompted the Mirditë men to remark, "He is saying mass now," while to the man being measured they would say:

"The gentleman is blessing you now, like the friar, so that you'll be immune to malaria. Pay close attention to his words."

When an old man came over to be measured, they teased him, saying:

"You are finished."

"You've come to a bad end."

"They will give you a set of false teeth."

They're drafting you in the army."

"They are going to fit you with new clothes from America. How do you want them, red or white?"

When a younger man was being measured, they made fun of him with remarks such as:

"Conduct yourself like a bridegroom, because they're taking you to America."

"They are shipping you a bride from America."

"He is weak; marriage, you see, has enfeebled him."[37]

"Sit down like a gentleman now. They're bringing you coffee, you know."

Men without hair on their body were given a rough time, so it is not surprising that they did not want to be measured in public. They were the butt of jokes like:

"His moustache was gobbled up by the devil."

"His wife left him."

"He is not quite a man."

"He is still too young to grow a moustache."

If a man had been afflicted by smallpox, they would say that a worm had eaten his face. And when a man with a glass eye showed up, they said that the doctors had replaced his eye with the eye of a dog.

A man had to have a perfect body; otherwise they would instantly find something to tease him about.

---

37 The popular belief in Albania at the time—a belief still alive in some quarters in America, as well—was that sexual intercourse weakened the male, but strengthened the female.

16

Mirditë Amusements

Both young and old in Mirditë play "*kësulash*" (hats), a game that can be played inside, as well as outside in the church courtyard. To play it, the players place several hats—sometimes sneaker sox—on the ground. Then they form themselves into two teams. Next, one of the teams hides a ring under one of the hats, and the trick is for the other team to find the ring, and to do so with no more than three tries at it. If it fails, the first team hides the ring again, and the opposing team tries again to take it away from them. The game continues until one side wins 100 points. If the game is played outside, the winners form a circle and begin to sing and dance, all the while making fun of the losers. The dancers link arms one with the other, and they dance in place rather than go around in a circle.

The game known as "*filxhanash*" (cups) is identical to the above. The difference is that the players in this case use coffee cups instead of hats or sneaker sox to play the game.

In some places we played cards with the local inhabitants after dinner. A game that in Korçë is known as *konçinë*, is called "*spathish*" in Mirditë. Here, the Jack has been christened "gendarme" by the highlanders, and in accordance with their way of playing game, can pick up all the cards on the table. Otherwise, there is not the slightest difference between this game and the *konçinë* that is played in the cities.

Children play a game known as *dojka*, which resembles that of *rakadoçe* in Tiranë. They play the game in front of their houses or in an open field. Holding each a stick with both hands, they hit a block of wood with it, while another kid tries to guide the block into a hole.[38] It is good exercise for them.

---

38 This game could be an ancient forerunner of the modern game of golf, inasmuch as it makes use of three important elements in golf: the stick, a "ball" or object to strike with the stick, and a hole for the ball.

Another Mirditë game is that of *rras*. In this game, the players divide into two parties, which face each other about ten meters apart. On the ground halfway between them is a row of stones in upright position. The object of the game is to knock the stones down. The party that knocks them down first wins, and as the reward the winners mount the back of the losers, and are given a ride from the losers' base back to their home ground. The game continues until both parties are exhausted.

The other games are *topthi* (ball) and *kala* (fortress), which in my opinion are no different from games played in other parts of Albania. These games are played by young and old at any time, but especially on feast days, above all on Easter Sunday.

One might suppose that the above games are the monopoly of Mirditë. But it is not true, as I have seen them played in other highland regions as well.

To change the subject now, do not think that the Mirditë highlander has a bad ear for music. When he plays the çifteli he captivates you, as the saying goes, even though he uses but a primitive instrument. The çifteli is played frequently, and is another form of amusement for the people. You see the highlander sitting cross-legged and moving his fingers rapidly over the neck of the guitar-like instrument. Around a singer of renown, other men stand or sit cross-legged, listening intently to the performer. The singer is ever ready to do encores for the sake of his listeners.[39] The songs may have a beautiful melody, but are somewhat long and repetitious. As a result, the simple melody becomes tiresome after a while. It seems that what the Mirditë highlander enjoys most are the lyrics rather than the melodies of the songs. To show their appreciation to the singer at the end of the performance, his listeners will say with one voice:

"Bless your voice! May your heart sing always!"

Other musical instruments used in Mirditë, besides the çifteli, are the *fyell* (shepherd's pipe), the *kavall* (fife), the *bilbil* (whistle) and the *zambare* (flute). I heard it said that the shepherd's pipe was what the

[39] The author is referring here to the venerable tradition of the epic folk singer, characteristic of northern Albania. The more renowned singers in this tradition could recite from memory hundreds of lines in a song, or what is more remarkable, sometimes improvised the lyrics as they sang.

Devil himself played, while Christ played the fife. They fashion the fife from the barrel of a long rifle. The whistle and the flute are made from green twigs, the first consisting of a single piece, and the second of two pieces. The flute has a reed that causes it to produce a thin sound like that of an oboe. A horn is attached at the end of the instrument to amplify the volume. At gatherings, instrumental music may be followed by vocal music, the quality of which depends on the skill of the singer. One can count on the fingers of the hand those who sing well and are the pride of the village. If asked, the natives will quickly tell you who sings well, and do not hesitate to call out his name, so that he may come over to you.

In martial times, target shooting was one of the favorite pastimes in the highlands. You can imagine the pride felt by the man who made his reputation as a sharpshooter! Today, however, they use stones instead of bullets to hit the target, achieving thus the same end, but in a different manner.

Games, songs, dances, instrumental music, etc., are not the only means used in Mirditë to make life more pleasant. Conversation also makes people forget themselves, especially talk of politics. Adults as well as children follow with keen interest the discussion of politics by the "experts." It is interesting to listen to such talk by the fireside or in the church courtyard. It seems as if the highlanders pick up the news of the day right out of thin air.

As for the politics of Europe, they claim to know it backward and forward. An expert will say, "England gave warning to Germany, but Germany was not frightened at all, because it is far the greatest power in Europe."

Another one cuts in with the observation: "It's true that Germany is the strongest power in Europe, but England is surrounded by water, and there is no way Germany can invade it. So they fight mostly in the air."

The children listen wide-eyed to these modern prophets, but make no comments, as it is improper for them to speak on such a subject!

Discussions center not only on world politics, but on stories of valor from the history of Mirditë. Naturally the elders boast about the grand old days, and relate to the youth tales about the old timers who fought to defend the faith and preserve the customs of the land. They tell how they fought against *Karadak* (Montenegro) and other enemies, beating them every time. They tell about the great bravery of a certain highlander who fought intrepidly against a large force of gendarmes. They tell about another one who brought honor upon himself and his kin by avenging the blood of his brother, etc., etc. Songs are sung about these men, and the young people, hearing such tales from the mouths of the elders, have attempted to emulate them, often at the risk of their lives.

Winter has its own charm, since at that time these rugged men and their children gather around the fireplace and tell riddles, fables, anecdotes, frightful tales (for example, a raid by a pack of wolves, the ordeal of crossing a raging river), and jokes which, added to the pastimes we mentioned previously, help to make the lives of the Mirditë people relatively happy.

17
Funeral Customs

When someone dies in Mirditë, a certain person known as "*thirrës morti*" (funeral messenger) informs the kinsfolk of the deceased, in accordance with instructions given to him by the family of the deceased. Friends of the family likewise are informed by word of mouth.

The kinsfolk then take over the management of the house of the departed, including the preparation of meals, the fetching of wood from the mountain and other chores. The members of the bereaved family do nothing but stay by the deceased, and lament his passing.

If the deceased is a female, her body is washed by the women; if a male he is washed by the men. Then they dress up the deceased in his best suit of clothes, cross his hands over the body, place a rosary with a cross in his hands, and lay him out on a wooden stand known as a "*vigj*." This stand is used to transport the body to the church where he is placed in a wooden coffin, provided by his family and the village.

The body is kept indoors at night, while in the daytime it is laid out in the courtyard. The mother, sisters and relatives take their places at the head of the *vigj*. Tallow candles burn above the head of the deceased.

Friends bring coffee on arriving at the house of the bereaved family.

A close relative will come with a ram or some other specimen of livestock. A nephew of the family does the same.

Upon entering the courtyard, women who come to pay their respects to the deceased say to members of the grieving family: "May the Lord give you strength."

To which the family members reply: "May you be strong and healthy."

Then the women sit down by the body and begin to weep. As soon as another group of women comes in, the first ones get up and go inside the house for a cup of coffee, while those who just arrived take their places. When men come into the yard, they put the hoods of their short-sleeved jackets on their head and yell:

"I am desolate my friend, desolate!"

Groaning "eh! eh! eh!", they kneel down by the deceased and kiss him. Then they get up and go inside for a cup of coffee. The same ritual may be observed by another group of men that may come in to express condolences.

Husbands do not weep for their departed wives, for they think it's unmanly to weep for women. However, the wife's brothers, sisters and relatives, including members of her husband's family, can lament her passing.

After a 24-hour wake, the kinsfolk and friends assemble in the morning and prepare to bury the deceased. Arriving with the body in the church, they transfer it from the wooden stand to the coffin, after first wrapping it up in a white cloth. The priest performs the last rites, and the body is then interred, fully clothed. In addition, the deceased carries a coin in his mouth, placed there so that he may be able to pay his debts in the other world. When the coffin is lowered in the grave, each one present throws a handful of earth over it, and at the same time says prayerfully:

"May the Lord receive him in paradise. May the Lord have mercy on his soul!"

If the deceased had not been to confession for a long time, or was guilty of a great crime, he is buried in an "unhallowed" plot of land rather than on hallowed ground.

After the burial, the funeral participants return to the home of the departed where they are served dinner. The meal consists of meat and rice, or a type of dish known as "blood and fat," made of corn flour, fat and the blood of slain animals, all mixed together and cooked. I heard that it's a very tasty dish. The meat is served separately. The men drink *raki* as they partake of hors d'oeuvres of fried liver and feta cheese.

As if the tears shed already for the deceased were not enough, he is lamented a second time at his home, just as if his body were still in the courtyard. They simulate his presence there by taking a suit of clothes and placing it over the spot where he lay, and then weep for him as before.

The same custom is observed in Mirditë on certain holidays as well. In Kalivar this occurs on St. John's Day; in Fan on St. Mark's Day.

The lament varies, depending on whether the deceased is young or old, whether he was slain of died a natural death. Following are a few lines from a lament in Mirditë, in which a mother pours out the pain of her heart over the loss of her son who was killed by another man because of his failure to pay a fine.

O bravest of the brave, oh my brave one!
Hey, you ferocious dog, oh my brave one!
Hey you light-winged eagle, oh my brave one!
You were looking for the Drin
  river and the sea, oh my brave one!
You roamed over the boundless sea, oh my brave one!
You roamed over the pathless mountain, oh my brave one!
Who could compare with you, oh my brave one!
Not just in looks alone, oh my brave one!
But in character, too, oh my brave one!

When the sun rose from the mountain, oh my brave one!
You made the sign of the cross, oh my brave one!
You threw your vest over the shoulder, oh my brave one!
When you reached the gate of the corral, oh my brave one!
You slung the rifle over your shoulder, oh my brave one!
You called out to the goats and rams, oh my brave one!
And led them across the meadow, oh my brave one!
To take them to the cool watering place, oh my brave one!

Ndue Kol Maroci stepped up to you, oh my brave one!
Demanding that you pay the fine, oh my brave one!
But since that you could not do, oh my brave one!
You turned your back on him, oh my brave one!
Then he shot you with his rifle, oh my brave one!
Like an oak tree you fell down, oh my brave one!

Neither of you shamed your kin, oh my brave one!
Both of you fell lifeless to the ground, oh my brave one!

Can it possibly be more beautiful? Laments such as this are not only a mirror of the soul of the grieving individual; they are a living history of the land from which they originate.

The visitors stay a long time after dinner is served. Upon leaving the house of the bereaved they will say to the head of the family:

"May we never come back again on sad occasions."

Friends who were not able to bring coffee with them, leave a money token for the family.

The priest may receive about twenty crown pieces, perhaps a lamb or sheep, or even an ox. They make much of donating an ox to the church!

No other memorial services are held for the departed. Only women friends make visits from time to time to the bereaved family to share its sorrow.

A young widow may marry within forty days following the death of her husband. But if she has children, she may, if she wishes, continue to live in her husband's home. In general, widows remarry, as they are much sought after.

18

Weddings

Engagements in Mirditë are made in infancy. Consequently, the boy and the girl do not have a chance to get to know each other before they marry. In the selection of the bride, consideration is given to whether or not she is of honorable lineage, the kind of parents she has, and whether she has a good uncle. Families are very eager to form marriage ties with honorable and powerful families, since by so doing they strengthen their own position. We can say therefore that the main object of marriage in Mirditë—like marriages among royalty and great families all over the world—is the mutual strengthening of the families concerned.

Generally speaking, the husband is older than the wife, but very often a widow will marry a man younger than herself. This may happen because there are no women in the man's household, and there is a need for an experienced woman in the house. Because they are more highly thought of, widows command a higher sum of money as well. For example, a man will pay 25 to 30 *qese* (50 to 60 *napolon* gold coins) for a young widow, while for a maiden he will pay 10 to 15 *qese* (20 to 30 napolon). The reason widows command a higher price is that they have been through thick and thin and are ready to handle any situation.

To seal the marriage contract, the head of the husband's house gives to the head of the bride's house a "*facoletë*" (handkerchief), 300 *grosh* (24 francs), and a "*myhyr*" (signet ring). These items are regarded as "*shenja*" (tokens) of the contract, and their acceptance is very significant. Returning them to the prospective groom, or failure to fulfill the agreement, is viewed as a great insult, and often ends in homicide.

If the girl does not wish to marry the man intended for her, her father returns the "tokens" to him. But in that case, the girl is forbidden to marry again, as long as the man she was supposed to marry is alive. Violation of this rule is perceived as a dishonorable deed, and the man's family may feel impelled to kill someone in the girl's household in order to remove the stain on the family's reputation.

The money for the bride is paid in installments, the balance being paid at the time of the wedding. The bride's father may, for example, ask the groom's father for payment of 100 *grosh* (8 francs) by a certain date. If the money is not paid by that date, he may impose a fine on him; that is, he may ask for an additional sum when he receives payment at a later date.

Weddings in Mirditë begin on Saturday, with the arrival of kinsfolk and friends. Daughters-in-law of the family arrive a week before the wedding and leave a week after the wedding ceremony.

The arrival of men guests is greeted with the firing of rifles at the gate. The women for their part sing the following lines:

Who comes here with a ram?
It's the mayor's deputy.
Does he bring us any gift?
Yes, he brings a lovely ram;
May the Lord increase his flock.

On Saturday the wedding guests eat beans, deep-fried dough, fish, rice, honey, pies, etc. The men drink *raki* and *kafe* (coffee).

The women sing their own songs; the men play the *tambura* (a three-string guitar-like instrument), as well as sing.

The same day, the head of the groom's household, together with about ten other wedding guests, set out for the house of the bride, taking with them the groom's ram, some four liters of *raki*, and four kg. of feta cheese. Once there, they amuse themselves with song and dance.

On Sunday, two hours before dawn, the wedding guests feast on the ram of the groom. Then the head of the bride's household brings over a huge, round loaf of bread to the father of the bridegroom, who proceeds to break off a piece from the loaf and says:

"Good luck! May the friendship between our families grow and bear fruit."

Then he asks the bride's father, "Are you ready?," at which point the latter presents the bride. The bride's father then asks for the 100 *korona* (crown pieces) due the bride's uncle, and the 100 crowns due the bride's brother. In case they don't give him the money, they are obliged to leave something behind as security.

The bride is escorted to her husband's home by her mother or some other woman. Her fine bridal outfit includes a red cap, a string of coins across her forehead, plus a red handkerchief. After packing the bridal chest, the bride is mounted on a horse, and together with the groom's party heads for her new home.

When she reaches the courtyard of her husband's home, her mother-in-law takes a bowl containing walnuts, sugar and wheat, and throws the contents into the air. After the bride dismounts the horse, a little boy walks three times under the belly of the horse. It is believed that this gesture will cause the bride to give birth to a boy! The bride then sits down on the threshold of her new home, while in the courtyard the wedding guests devour the huge bridal loaf of bread that was given to the groom's party earlier by the bride's father.

While the guests are dancing, someone may break in and say:

Two sheep and three hundred coins,
He who does not get up to dance,
May his wife elope this very night.

On Monday or Tuesday the bride and groom are wed in the village church. The *kumbare* (best man) accompanies the bride to church for confession. Two *kumbare*[40] assist the crowning of the couple, one standing to the right of the bride, the other to the left of the groom. They place their right hand on the shoulder of the groom, and the left hand on the shoulder of the bride. Then the priest takes the ring from the bride's finger, blesses it and gives it to the bridegroom who slips it on her finger. The priest now says to the groom:

"Do you accept this woman for your wife?"

He answers "Yes." The priest poses the same question to the bride, who is embarrassed to reply. After the ceremony the people leave the church and set out for the groom's house. The groom's father leads the way, followed by the bridegroom, the *kumbares*, the bride and her mother-in-law, and finally the kinsfolk and friends.

---

40 The two *kumbare* here are the equivalent of the "best man" and the "maid of honor" in an American wedding.

A ten-year-old boy now takes the bride to the village fountain to draw water. She fills a pitcher with water, and upon returning home pours for everyone in the house, so they may wash their hands. To the youngest boy she gives a pair of laces for his sandals. Throughout this ritual she is careful to pour water not in drip-drip fashion, but in a steady stream.

In the evening, a little boy takes the bride's sandals off, and inside them he finds a crown that she had placed there just before leaving her maternal home.

When the wedding is over, each guest leaves a present on the dining table, according to what he can afford. One guest may leave two crowns, another three, and still another more than three.

As they prepare to depart, all those who came with rams form a line in the courtyard. The bride then gives each one a pair of sox for a present. She places the present on their shoulder. To the women she gives tasseled waistbands.

After this ceremony the guests return home. The groom's mother-in-law also departs, leaving the bride and the groom alone. There is a taboo against the groom visiting his mother-in-law's house, either before or after the wedding. This is seen more clearly in the following lines:

> Who is purer than a dove?
> The nephew at his uncle's home.
> Who is blacker than the raven?
> The groom at his wife's home.

In olden times the Mirditë bridegroom never set foot in the house of his mother-in-law. Now however he visits her three or four months after the wedding.

Three days after the wedding, the groom sends his bride to her mother loaded with bread, pies, etc., in order to "clear the way." She stays there overnight, then returns with a tray heaped up with twice as much food as she brought over to her mother. As time passes, the bride accustoms herself to the new life in her husband's home.

With the 15 *qese* (600 francs) the bride receives from her husband-to-be, she prepares her trousseau, including the crown and the other things needed for the wedding. When she comes to her new home, she also brings presents for her husband, father-in-law and mother-in-law, brothers-in-law and sisters-in-law, and for the aunts of the family. The presents may be such articles as sox, sneaker sox, handkerchiefs and other things.

As for the sox that the bride gives to the guests who come with sheep, the groom's mother informs the bride's mother well in advance, so as to allow enough time for the knitting of the sox.

Considering that a girl in Mirditë brings a good sum of money, one would think that girls would be more desirable than boys. Yet, that is not how things stand. Certain sayings in Mirditë indicate the very opposite. Note for instance the following: "The house and its beams weep when a girl is born into it."

The reason for this belief is that a daughter eventually leaves the house and settles in another home, whereas a son stays and fathers new offspring, thus insuring the continuation of the family line.

We have said in this chapter that the girl who returns the "tokens" of the engagement to her would-be-husband, must not marry as long as he is alive. In that case, the woman is called a virgin, and she may even dress like a man. A woman may remain a virgin also as a result of a bodily defect, which makes her unsuitable for marriage. In Fan we met a 22-year-old girl who said she was going to remain a virgin. When I asked her why, she told me that she did not care to marry the man to whom she had been engaged, preferring instead to remain at home and take care of her aged father and her only brother. In other words, she was sacrificing her life for her father and brother. In case a girl in her position dishonors herself,[41] her brother, father, or a close relative would be obliged to kill her to wipe off the stain on the family's honor. Long live the bullet!

---

[41] A dishonorable act in this context would be for her to have sexual relations with another man.

19

The Blood Feud

Blood feuds in Mirditë are the result of a number of things: the absence of a government strong enough to administer justice in the region; the primitive notion that justice could be carried out by the injured party himself; the pride of the Mirditë man and of the highlander in general which renders him unable to endure an insult or forget an injury, and to respond instead according to the principle of a "tooth for a tooth;" and the self-interest of clan leaders who derived a good income from their efforts at reconciling feuding parties. Blood feuds, the Curse of our Highlands, have existed in Mirditë until recent times. Today "feuds" are the responsibility of the Government, and following the collection of arms in possession of the citizenry, shooting incidents have dropped sharply. Anyone can now travel in these remote areas in safety.

"Before, you didn't dare step out your front door, for fear of getting killed!," the men of Mirditë told me when the subject came up. "Now there is peace, and the people can take their livestock to the mountains, or work in their fields."

What a change!

Kanuni i Lekës (The Law of Lekë) spelled out in its articles the punishment to be meted out to a person who committed an injustice, and the damages, which were assessed by the elders, involved a certain compensation, but not the use of guns. Shootings occurred as a result of insults to one's father and mother, the slaying of a guest, questions of honor,[42] elopement, the burning down of one's house, stealing of livestock, etc. Minor offenses, such as the cutting off of irrigation water, tampering with border marker stones on farm property, etc., which could have been settled amicably by the elders, very often led to shootings. Incidents of this kind were due to hot tempers, and to

42 In the Albanian idiom, questions of honor involved, among others, affronts to one's personal dignity, besmirching of the reputation of one's family or kin, and violations of the sexual code regarding women.

a smaller extent, the dissatisfaction of one or the other disputant with the verdict of the elders.

The shooting could occur immediately in the course of a quarrel, or at an ambush set by the wronged party either by himself or in collaboration with friends, and lastly by hiring an assassin to do the job. The most honorable way of settling accounts with one's enemy was to confront him face to face.

When a shooting occurred, the code of honor required that the killer inform the family of the victim about the incident, in order to avoid the subsequent shooting of an innocent party. The family and kin of the killer then had to be on guard for 24 hours, because they could be killed at any time during that period by a member of the killer's kinsfolk. It did not matter whether the victim of revenge was an infant or an old man. Only the women were exempt from revenge.

After 24 hours, only the killer himself or a male member of his family was subject to shooting. The family of the victim lived in disgrace as long as it did not wash off the stain on its honor by taking the life of a member of the enemy household. The revenge seeker was a social outcast as long as he did not avenge the blood of the victim, because wherever he went, people talked about him, and regarded him as a coward if he was slow in taking revenge. To show their contempt for such a person at a wedding, say, or a party, they filled his glass of whiskey only half full, and shook hands with him with the left instead of with the right hand. In other words, society itself, because, of its evil customs, often was the cause of new shootings. After all, it is no little matter to a highlander to be called a coward and to be abused at every turn. Even if he had no intention to kill, such group mentality depresses a man to the point of making him commit the disgusting deed.

Let us suppose that someone in the killer's family was killed, and the blood of the original victim avenged. What happened then? The mutual search for revenge continued, and eventually could bring about the ruin of both families. Continuous warfare caused great harm to both parties since, apart from the loss of life, the men involved in the feud could not work freely. For this reason, friends of the two feuding parties would intervene and bring about a *besëlidhje* (truce)[43] which for a certain length of time guaranteed freedom and security to the killer. Friends and mediators who approached the victim's family in order to arrange a truce did not receive any payment. The truce of the village lasted for thirty days. If the truce was broken during this period, both the contracting parties and the mediators were held responsible for it. The truce was thus an essential institution in the Highlands, and the house that became a party to it, regarded its participation as an act of bravery and honor.

But the truce was in force for only a short period of time, after which the blood-shedding resumed. Knowing this, people of goodwill interceded to bring about a total reconciliation between them. In this instance, too, the mediators bore full responsibility if the victim's family caused the taking of a life in the family of the assailant.

Blood feuds in Mirditë could not be ended through payment of money. The families that became parties to such a deal were held in contempt by society. When a deal of that kind did take place, the family of the victim received 12 *napolona* (240 francs) from the assailant, in return for its consent to end the feud; and half as much if the victim were a woman. This does not mean that life was cheap in Mirditë. The money was given by the assailant as a "token" of his sincerity, and in addition served as a form of security for him. The negotiators of the reconciliation received 100 *grosh* (8 francs) per person.

The arrival for the first time of the killer into the house of the victim must have been a heart-rending experience. Just imagine the first moments of the meeting between the killer and the head of the victim's household in the men's parlor. What wrenching emotional struggles must have taken place within the soul of the latter. To face the man who wiped off the face of the earth his loved one! Yet, he can

---

43 The *besëlidhje* means pledging one's faith or word of honor in a verbal agreement that has a binding force far above any written contract. The *besëlidhje,* which generally means "alliance," has as its root the word *besë,* commonly regarded as the supreme virtue in the Albanian code of ethics. Actually, the *besë* is the composite of virtues or character traits encompassing honor, faith, trust, and loyalty. Indeed, *besa e Shqiptarit* (the Albanian's faith) has had practically the force and authority of a religion.

do nothing, except embrace him and say to him, "Welcome, oh friend!," because the custom demands it.

Even if his heart is broken, the head of the house is obliged to attend the party given by his family to mark the end of the feud and the beginning of peace. At the end of the party they take an adz and carve out a cross with it on the outside door of the house, to prevent any act of treachery and insure success of the reconciliation effort.

The foregoing procedure applied to the settlement of feuds between families only. It must have been horrifying when the feud involved two villages or even two clans. In that case, collective warfare brought about a general paralysis of the normal life of the belligerents. How could a people that lived in such circumstances progress? Until a truce could be arranged, the blood feud flowed ceaselessly, and the side that killed the most people boasted about this act of valor!

A blood feud had the potential to continue "ad infinitum." That is why it was necessary for the leaders to get together and call a truce. Nor should we forget that a truce occurred also when times called for unity in order to achieve a common goal. It was essential at such times to put aside their enmities in order to deal effectively with the challenge posed by the common enemy.

There was no specified time as to when a general reconciliation of feuds could take place. It could happen once every 4 or 5 years, according to need. After the reconciliation there was a period of quiet. However, a condition of peace was not beneficial to the Highland leaders, as it went against their interests (inasmuch as they received a certain compensation for the settlement of every feud); consequently, the tragic cycle of the blood feud resumed.

The family that took a life after the declaration of a general truce was heavily punished. For example, its house was burned down and its orchard destroyed; it could be expelled from the *bajrak* for two to three years; and 100 sheep and an ox could be confiscated from its livestock as payment of a fine. The booty of the fine was distributed among the leaders of the community. If the victim were a woman, the fine imposed on the offending family was half as much.

It is fortunate that at present "blood feuds" are the responsibility of the Government which looks out for the welfare of the country. The feud mentality has not disappeared the chance to do so. Those who are subject to the tradition of the blood feud must be made aware of their condition, for only when they see clearly the evil fruits of the blood feud mentality will they cease to live by the principle of "a tooth for a tooth." In addition, they must have more trust in the Government, whose chief aim is to serve the people with justice. Decent Government representatives can undoubtedly do much to strengthen this trust, seeing that it is so essential in our Highland regions.

20
A Few Songs

In an earlier chapter I mentioned that the Mirditë highlander enjoys singing, and has a special liking for song lyrics. Further on are a number of songs on different subjects which I hope the reader will find interesting, especially since folk songs mirror the life and soul of the people from whose bosom they derive. Before we discuss these particular songs, it would not be a bad idea to make some general observations about folk songs.

The subject and form of folk songs are always simple. This is natural, and one should expect this of a place where social life has not been influenced by civilization with all its complications.

Although it was created by an individual artist, the folk song is the property of all, rather than the property of its originator. This may have happened in the following manner: An event of importance took place in the region (let us say, a fight between two brave warriors, and so on), and quickly the unknown poet, in order to sanctify the event, composed a song, which he then perhaps sang to his fellow villagers in an open field, or perhaps in the church courtyard. Having won the hearts of everybody, the song spread from person to person, and finally became the property of the people. In time, the name of its creator was forgotten, and each subsequent singer added, subtracted of changed parts of the song to suit his taste. For example, I found that the Song of Zanë—a popular name in Mirditë—is also sung in Shosh in the Dukagjin region, but in a different form.

The above example shows that a song not only changes in content, but travels as well from one place to another. Each place alters the song in accordance with its own character, and this very fact makes it difficult to trace its origin.

Unlike other verse compositions, these songs are not vehicles of personal expressions of the feelings and thoughts of their creators. They express instead the general feelings and thoughts of the group, whose soul they mirror. Folk songs are impersonal.

Even though they are simple in every respect, folk songs are very beautiful, for they contain poetic words and expressions that touch the heart. They are infused with the poetic spirit. They are not colorless and dry, like certain modern poems, which are merely a rhythmic arrangement of words.

It has been noted that the majority of folks songs have a refrain, that is, words and phrases that have already appeared in the song. For example, in songs of lament we have the refrain, "*O trimthi jem! O meku jem!*" (Oh, my brave one! Oh my friend!), whereas in the song of Gjin Lekë,

Vrau nji beg të Tepelis,
Vrau nji beg, nji beg të ran

(He shot a bey [44] of Tepelis,
He shot a bey of prestige)

we have a repetition of phrase. This is done for emphasis, but it may also be due to the primitive nature of this kind of poetry.

Let us now look at the songs given below. The first is the song of Zanë, which was prompted by the loss of two brothers. The monologue of Zanë is very beautiful, filled with poetic expressions that cannot be improved upon.

Në ju qyqja mos kënoftë,
Në ju lulja mos lulzoftë

(May the cuckoo bird never sing here,
May flowers never bloom here)

These are powerful lines of malediction. Even so, one feels compassion for this unfortunate bride when she says:

Unë s'kjeshë nuse për m'u gëzue,
Por kjeshë zanë për me u zanue!

(I was not meant to be a happy bride,
But a fairy living under a spell!)

---

44 Turkish honorary title, designating a nobleman.

Although I tried to collect a few love songs, I was not able to do so, because whenever I asked the highland men about such songs, they would reply, “We don’t know women’s songs.” They thought it was shameful for a man to recite a love song, instead of songs of valor. The few love songs I did find were banal and do not merit publication. One that was fairly good is included here. It is a pleasant piece characterized by unity of ideas, and tells a story that may have happened. The dialogue is interesting, especially the final lines spoken by the girl to her mother:

Me pas kenë mori nanë ti,
Të kish lujt mënnja sot në pleqni!

(Had you been there, mother dear,
You’d have lost your head, despite your years!)

Laments reveal the pain of the person who has lost a loved one, and contain phrases that can break the heart of the listener. The mourner first says:

E zgjodhi pikën e djalit,
I shkrini në bark të zjarmit!

(He chose the cream of youth,
And threw their lives away!)

Later a lamenting singer uses the melancholic phrases:

Jon’ nnez qirat s’kanë bâ drit, o trimthi jem!
Këmanat kanë ra por mesht s’janë pa, o trimthi jem!

(The candles were lit, but shed no light,
oh my brave one!
The church bells tolled,
but no masses were celebrated,
oh, my brave one!)

It is by means of those contrasts that the mourner has been able to reveal the dimensions of the great misfortune that has occurred. The repetition of the refrain adds to the melancholy of the lament.

I have noticed that the majority of the songs I heard in Mirditë have bravery as their theme. It could be the bravery of an individual, as in the case of the songs reproduced here, or collective bravery which sings of the valor of all of Mirditë. Three of the songs reproduced here are examples of individual bravery, as manifested in different circumstances. In these songs we see the revelation of true manliness, conveyed by means of words such as,

> *S'e nap pushkën sa të jet jeta!*
>
> (I won't surrender as long as I live!)

and:

> *Bini djelm no' i t'a mysim,*
> *Të nnerojmë vedin e t'nnerojm fisin!*
>
> (Fire at them, boys, and mow them down,
> To honoring ourselves and our kin!)

Nnue Marku, a young man, leaves the following mandate to his mother:

> *E mos lisho gjâm*
> *Se kam dhan jetën*
> *E s'kam dhan gjân*
> *Edhe marre prapa nuk kam lanë*
>
> (And do not weep for me
> I only gave my life, you see
> I did not give up what's mine
> No shameful name leave I behind.)

The brave warrior died so as not to disgrace his home and himself. For insulting the father and mother of the dashing Gjin Leke, Adem paid with his life. How could a man like Gjin ignore an insult of that nature, he who had been trained

> *Me hek alltien dhe të tri herat me i ba nji?*
>
> (To fire three shots from his revolver
> so fast that they sounded like one shot?)

The golden-tongued poet closes his song with these lines of glorious praise for the hero:

Ke bjen djelli e ke bjen hana,
Si Gjin Lekën s'e ban ma nana,
As n'beglerë as n'Kapidana.

(Nowhere on this earth of ours,
Shall woman again give birth to another Gjin Leke,
Not even among families of *beys* and *kapedans*.)

Song No. 1

There was an old woman with two orphaned boys,
She went around begging and pleading,
For food to feed the boys,
She wanted to raise them like men;
When they reached the age of twenty,
The two boys asked the old woman:
"What sort of work did father do?"
"Upon my word, I'll tell you,
My son did marvelous deeds,
With passion he hunted in the mountains,
And it was there that he died;
And his dying words to me were:
A curse on hunting in the mountains."
The two boys thought long and hard,
Long and hard, and then decided.
Both bought guns in the market place,
And set off riding on a donkey,
Followed by a pack of street hounds;
When they reached the lofty mountain,
They met and old man with a woman,
The old man sang as he walked,
His *nuse* followed with tearful eyes.
And through her tears the *nuse* said:
"Dry up you mountains all around,
You offer no shade to the traveler,
Nor water to quench his thirst;
May you never know the cool of shade;

May spring water never well up from you,
May the cuckoo bird never sing here,
May the flowers never bloom here.
How is it no hunter ever showed up,
To slay this old man and marry me?"
The two boys thought long and hard,
Long and hard, and then decided,
With both rifles they shot the old man,
And took his bride along with them.
Then brother quarreled with brother.
Says one, the woman is mine,
Says the other, never, never,
Says one, I'm your older brother,[45]
Says the other, you won't have her while I live;
The first then shot his brother dead,
And took the bride for himself.
But the woman started scolding:
Says she, "The Lord has made you mad,
To kill your brother for a woman,
For sure, your friends will scorn you,
Soon as your mother sees me,
Because the boy died for me."
The boy thought long and hard,
Long and hard and then decided,
He fired a bullet in his head.
The unhappy *nuse* then cried out:
"I was not meant to be a happy bride,
But a fairy living under a spell."

Song No. 2

Two pretty ones go to the fountain,
One a maiden, the other a bride.
"Stay, maiden, and speak to me,
And cause the woman to like me."
"Come now, young man, what do you mean?
Why want her when you can have me?"

---

45 According to Albanian tradition, brothers in a family married in accordance with the seniority rule; that is, the older brother had the right to marry first.

Mother asked me why was I late?
"The water, mother, was all dirty,
With my handkerchief I had to strain it;
A boy with a çifteli was there,
And truly well he sang of love."
"Take care, lest young men deceive you."
"I swear, mother, I know nothing about that,
But had you heard him, mother dear,
You'd have lost your head, despite your years."

Song No. 3

The times are rough, o my brave one!
For shooting firearms, o my brave one!
The government officials fell, o my brave one!
Since the outlaws appeared, o my brave one!
Since the fool of Selice town appeared, o my brave one!
Since Llusku of Mirditë appeared, o my brave one!
And Çaba of Kacinari, o my brave one!
Koreci of Gojan, o my brave one!
Logja and Petoku of river Fan, o my brave one!
A curse on the house of Gjon Marku; o my brave one!
He rounded them up from far and near, o my brave one!
He chose the cream of youth, o my brave one!
And threw their lives away, o my brave one!
Why did not the sea swell up, o my brave one!
And turn back the boats out there? o my brave one!
You were brought up, o my brave one!
To drink of the rushing waters, o my brave one!
Not the stinking muddy kind; o my brave one!
It is now seven years, o my brave one!
Since the Pasha and his aids appeared, o my brave one!
There has not been one feast day, o my brave one!
The candles were lit, but shed no light, o my brave one!
The church bells tolled, o my brave one!
But no masses were celebrated, o my brave one!
When the Pasha came to Shpal, o my brave one!
He called a meeting of all Mirditë and asked, o my brave one!
That every home send him a fighting man, o my brave one!
And everyone obeyed his call, o my brave one!
The news then spread throughout Albania, o my brave one!

The men had been sent to Serbia, o my brave one!
The letters sent to them came back, o my brave one!
Pity the mothers who gave them birth! o my brave one!

Song No. 4

When you enter the Beyond, o my friend!
And they ask you about us, o my friend!
Say all but the sun and moon has changed, o my friend!
All the youth are in the army, o my friend!
They are dressed in army uniforms, o my friend!
They've taught them to speak Italian, o my friend!
They wear belts and bands and straps, o my friend!
They carry guns with bayonets, o my friend!

Song No. 5

In Istanbul the papers said,
Noc Mar Deda has declared,
"I shall fight as long as I live,
As long as I live I won't give up,
I'm determined to wipe out,
All the gendarmes chasing me."
The young man, Mustaf Asllani,
Grabbed a rifle, grabbed a pistol,
He wants to enter Berish town.
The night is dark, the terrain rough.
And finding Noc's house could be tough.
When they came to Noc's door,
A corporal with seven aids said:
"Noc Mar, step out to the door,
Step out to the door to talk to me;
We are sent here by the Kajmakam,[46]
To take you alive, not to harm you."
Noc has five minutes to decide.
The night, he notes, is a holy one,
Stepping out, Noc said a prayer:
Help me, O Night of St. Nicholas,

46 The *Kajmakam* was head of an administrative unit in the days of Turkish rule in Albania; the equivalent roughly of a prefect.

Help me Lord to hold my ground,
To kill these gendarmes, and then escape;
I'm not worried about father,
His time has come to die,
He has lived one hundred years.
"Fire at them, boys, we've slain Hidrizin,
Fire at them, boys, and mow them down,
Thus honoring ourselves and our kin!"

Song No. 6

That young man, Nnue Marku,
He grabs an ax, and with some goats,
Sets out for the Gjajmi pass.
The Selite army has been alerted,
And half of it is after me,
Hoping to catch me by mid-day;
I'm not armed with a rifle,
Being so young they wouldn't give it to me,
A dagger the length of two palms of the hand,
I gave to one of my best friends,
Gave him my lodge as well;
Another dagger I have with me,
Strapped securely by my leg.
Hear my dying words, oh mother,
When our livestock come home tonight,
Go and count them by the gate,
And do not weep for me,
I only gave my life you see,
I did not give up what's mine,
No shameful name leave I behind.

Song No. 7

The seven *kralat* wanted to know,
All about Gjin Lekë's deed.
In the other chamber of the *Vali's*[47] palace,
He shot a *bey* of Tepelis,
He shot a *bey* of prestige.
Losing no time, the *Vali,*
Met with Gjin and shook his hand:
Who told you to do this deed?
Said Gjin: "*Tunjatjeta, oh, Vali*,
One thing I have to say to you,
Adem[48] accused me of thievery,
Such a thing is foreign to me,
To me and my people, too.
When he insulted my father and mother,
He insulted Christ who made them.
Said I, 'Adem, it's wrong to speak ill of others,
It's a sin against the Lord,
To insult my parents as you did,'
The ground shook under my feet,
I drew my pistol and pulled the trigger,
The three shots sounding like one,
Flaming shots they were, all three,
And poor Adem dropped down dead.
Red was the cobblestone ground with his blood,
Red with his blood was the cobblestone ground."
Who was it, Lord, who fought this fight?
None other than the dashing Gjin;
Such are the young men of Gojani,
Of Gojani and the whole realm.
Had Gjin had a rifle on him,
A shambles he would have made of the town,
And amazed the whole world.
Nowhere on this earth of ours,
Shall woman again give birth to another Gjin Lekë,
Not even among families of *beys* and *Kapedans.*

---

47 The *Vali* was governor of a large province under the Turkish system of government.

48 Presumably the name of the *bey* shot by Gjin.

Biographical Sketch

COON, Carleton Stevens 1904-1981

Born June 23, 1904, in Wakefield, MA, died of cancer June 3, 1981, in Gloucester, MA. Anthropologist, educator and author. Considered one of the last great general anthropologist, Coon made contributions to many areas of the science. He studied the social anthropologies of contemporary societies, but his main interest was ancient man. Conducting both archeological and biological studies, the anthropologist traced the development of man from its earliest form to its agricultural society. In addition, he studied human adaptations to extreme environments, and he fostered a theory of race which purported that the five races of man evolved differently at different times and in different places. Coon conducted studies of primitive tribal groups currently living in the Middle East and in Patagonia, and led expeditions which unearthed 150,000-year-old bones of a Neanderthal man as well as some bones of a Stone Age Hotu man. A professor at Harvard and at the University of Pennsylvania, Coon became the curator of ethnology at the University Museum in Philadelphia, and he was also associated with the Peabody Museum of Archeology and Ethnology in Massachusetts. He was awarded the Legion of Merit, the Viking Medal in Physical Anthropology, and the Philadelphia Athenaeum Award.

His writings: *Tribes of the Rif,* Harvard University Press, 1931; *Flesh of the Wild Ox,* Morrow, 1932; *The Riffian,* Little 1933; *Measuring Ethiopia*, Little, 1934; *The Races of Europe,* Macmillan, 1939; (with E. D. Chapple) *Principles of Anthropology,* Henry Holt, 1942; (editor) *A Reader in General Anthropology,* Henry Holt, 1948; (with S.M. Garn and J. Birdsell) *Races,* C.C. Thomas, 1949; *The Mountains of Giants,* Peabody Museum Papers, Harvard University Press, 1949, *Caravan,* Henry Holt, 1953, 2nd edition, 1962; *The Seven Caves,* Knopf, 1957; *The Origin of Races,* Knopf 1962.

(From *Contemporary Authors*,
Vols. 5-8, 1969, p. 246, and Vol. 104, 1982, p. 91.)

Glossary of Words and Phrases

Following is a glossary of Albanian words and phrases appearing in the book, together with their English translations. In parentheses, immediately following the entries, are given the phonetic transcriptions for the English-speaking reader. However, since Albanian has a number of letters or sounds not found in English alphabet, these phonetic renderings are approximate rather than exact transcriptions. To indicate stress, the syllable on which the stress falls in the transcribed entries is in capital letters.

Allti (ahl-TEE)	revolver
Bajrak (by-RAHK)	administrative unit
Bajraktar (by-rahk-TAR)	head of a bajrak
Beg (beg)	bey (Turkish honorary title)
Besëlidhje (bess-LEE-thye)	truce; pledge of faith
Dallap (dah-LAHP)	type of revolver
Dita e Mirë (DEE-tah ey Meer)	The Good Day
Dojka (DOY-kah)	type of children's game
Dyshkë (DUE-shkuh)	old Turkish coin
Ethet e Gushtit (Ehthet eh GOO-shteet)	malarial fever of August
Facoletë (fah-tso-LEH-tuh)	type of kerchief
Falemneries (fah-lehm'-NAI-ri-yus)	thank you
Filxhanash (fil-JAH-nahsh)	cups (type of game)
Fyell (FUE-ell)	shepherd's pipe
Grosh (grohsh)	type of old currency
Halia (Hah-LEE-ah)	collective body for settling disputes, composed of one man per household
Hinkë (HIN-kuh)	funnel
Hute (HOO-tuh)	rifle

Internati (Een-tair-NAH-tee)	boarding school
Jo (yo)	no
Kafe (kah-FAY)	coffee
Kajmakan (Kye-mah-KAHN)	administrator in the Turkish government, roughly equal to a prefect
Kala (kah-LAH)	fortress (type of game)
Kanuni i Lekës (Kah-NOO-nee ee LEH-khus)	The Law of the Lek
Kapedan (Kah-peh-DAHN)	clan leader
Karadak (Kah-rah-DAHK)	Turkish word for Montenegro
Karajfile (kah-rye-FEE-leh)	type of flintlock gun
Kavali (kah-vah-LEE)	fife
Kësulash (kuh-SOO-lahsh)	hats (type of game)
Konçinë (kohn-CHEE-nuh)	type of card game
Koronë (koh-ROH-nuh)	crown (type of currency)
Kral (krahl)	(Serbian) king
Kullë (KOO-luh)	typical house in northern Albania
Kumbare (koo-MBAH-reh)	best man
Magjar (mah-GYAHR)	Hungarian
Mal i Shënjtë (Mahl ee SHUHNY'-tuh)	Sacred Mountain
Martinë (mahr-TEE-nuch)	Martin rifle
Mazere (mah-ZAI-reh)	Mauser rifle
Meze (meh-ZEH)	appetizer
Mirë (MEE-ruh)	fine, good, well
Mirë-Dita (meer'-DEE-tah)	Good Day
Nagane (nah-GAH-neh)	type of six-chambered revolver
Napolonë (nah-poh-LOH-nuh)	a gold coin, formerly worth 20 francs
Nuse (NOO-say)	bride; (loosely) daughter-in-law
Okë (OH-kuh)	measuring unit equaling 1.4 kg.
Oshxheldën (ohsh-JELL-dun)	Welcome
Para (Pah-RAH)	old Turkish currency
Petull (PEH-tool)	ball of batter fried in oil

Pite me Hinjth (PEE-teh meh hiny'th)	type of vegetable pie
Pite me kungull (PEE-teh meh KOO-ngool)	pumpkin pie
Pushkë (POO-shkuh)	rifle
Pushk' e gjatë (POO-shk eh GYAH-tuh)	long rifle
Pushkë llatine (POO-shkuh lah-TEE-neh)	Latin rifle
Qafë e Shënjtë (Chahf eh SHUHNY'-tuh)	Sacred Pass
Qese (CHEH-seh)	formerly, a sum of money equaling 40 francs
Rakadoçe (rah-kah-DOH-cheh)	type of children's game
Raki (rah-KEE)	clear brandy
Rras (rahs)	type of game
Shalë (SHAH-luh)	harness
Shefteli (chef-teh-LEE)	a stringed musical instrument
Shejshane (shay-SHAH-neh)	type of firearm
Shëmëria (Shuh-muh-REE-ya)	St. Mary
Shoshë (SHOH-shuh)	sieve
Shpatë (Shpah-tuh)	sword
Shputa (SHPOO-tah)	slipper sox
Shtatë kralat (SHTAH-tuh KRAH-laht)	the seven kings
Shumë mirë (SHOO-muh MEE-ruh)	very nice
Sofër (SOH-fur)	low, round dining table
Spathish (spah-THEESH)	type of card game
Tambura (Tah-mboo-RAH)	a three-stringed guitar-like instrument
Thirrës morte (THEE-ruhs MOHR-the)	funeral messenger
Topthi (TOHP-thee)	type of ball game
Tungjatjeta (Too-ngyaht-YEH-tah)	popular greeting meaning, "A long life to you."

*Urdhnoni (*Oorth-NOH-nee)	"Come in" (plural form; also polite form when used with single person)
Vali (Vah-LEE)	governor of a province in the Turkish administration
Vigj (veej)	bier
Xhami (jah-MEE)	mosque
Zambare (zah-MBAH-reh)	flute

A Gheg man posing for the photographer beside his oxen-drawn cartload

A different type of the Gheg

Portrait of the Gheg Albanian man

One member of the expedition

A typical Albanian Highlander
wearing a kerchief around the cap and neck

Mrs. Coon dressed in Gheg women's clothing (bodice)
and wearing with the brimless conical felt cap

Woman with two children bedecked with strings of trinkets, characteristic of the attire of women in Mirditë

View of street and dwellings in Northern Albania, showing the rough and cluttered character of the structures

Country scene with woodlands and a lonely *kullë*

Scene of a *kullë* (tower), a fortress-like home found in Mirditë and elsewhere in northern Albania

View of a majestic mountain peak in the Mirditë region,
one of many such peaks in the highlands